KU-168-807

THE
Elders
EXPLOSION

THE

EXPLOSION

One hundred and fifty years of
progress from Elder to Elliott

TIM HEWAT

BAY BOOKS
Sydney and London

Also by Tim Hewat:

The Comet Riddle

War File

DeGaulle File

Rollings Stones File

Advertising in Australia

The Plastics Revolution

Bridge Over Troubled Waters

The Champions

The Garryowen

The Blues

Golden Fleeces — The Falkiner Years at Boonoke

Golden Fleeces 11 — The Murdoch Years at Boonoke

The Intelligent Investor's Guide to Share Buying

Don Chipp — A Profile (with David Wilson)

This book is copyright. Apart from any fair dealing for the purpose of private study, research, criticism or review, as permitted under the Copyright Act, no part may be reproduced by any process without written permission. Enquiries should be addressed to the publishers.

Published by Bay Books, 61–69 Anzac Parade, Kensington, NSW 2033

Copyright © Tim Hewat

First published 1988

National Library of Australia
Card number and ISBN 1 86256 330 6

Designed by Chris Hatcher

Typesetting by Savage Type Pty Ltd, Brisbane

Printed in Adelaide by The Griffin Press

BB88

Contents

Money Note

Measuring a company's performance over a span of 150 years means that one is talking about money. But money changes. Its value is distorted by inflation. Indeed, money in Australia had its name and structure changed in 1966 when we switched from the pound, made up of 240 pence, to the dollar with 100 cents. Therefore, to write that a loaf of bread cost threepence sixty years ago, which it probably did, is meaningless to today's readers. What is the value in dollars and cents of something that cost threepence so long ago? In fact, it is 50 cents.

I am indebted to my friend Richard FitzHerbert, a Fellow of the Institute of Actuaries and managing director of Contrarian Management, who, for a book on the wool industry some years ago, calculated a conversion table based on historical statistics which enabled me to express old prices in modern values. His updated table and an explanation of his method is included as an appendix at the back of this book.

In the text, when I record that Thomas Elder launched a party of exploration in 1891 with a donation of five thousand pounds, it is expressed like this: £5,000 ($350,000)—the figures in brackets being today's value in dollars for the five thousand pounds.

I thank Richard for allowing me once again to employ this extremely useful converter.

Tim Hewat
Poplars Farm, 1988

John Elliott

Elders IXL Directors 1988

Left to right: *David I. Darling,
John M. Baillieu, Kenneth R.
Biggins, Geoffrey F. Lord, S.
Baillieu Myer, Alan G. McGregor,
Ian M. McLachlan, Gerald M.
Niall.*

Inset: O. Robert Gunn,

Left to right: Edmund A. Burton, Peter T. Bartels, Michael R. Nugent, Kenneth C. Jarrett, Charles R. Faggotter, Peter D. Scanlon.

Inset: Hon. Sir Edward Williams.

Company History

Some of the greatest names in Australian, British and Canadian commercial history formed the roots from which Elders has developed.

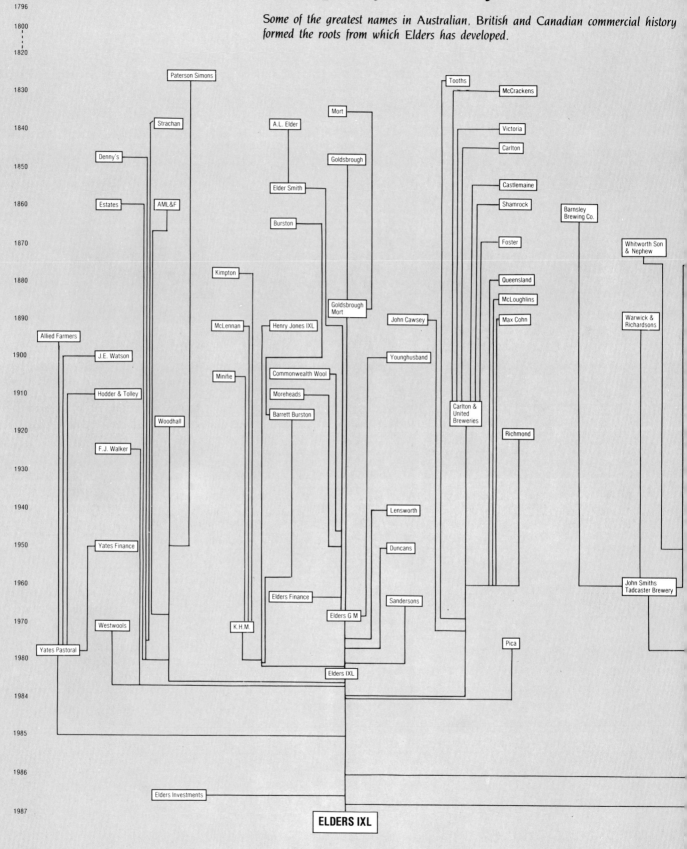

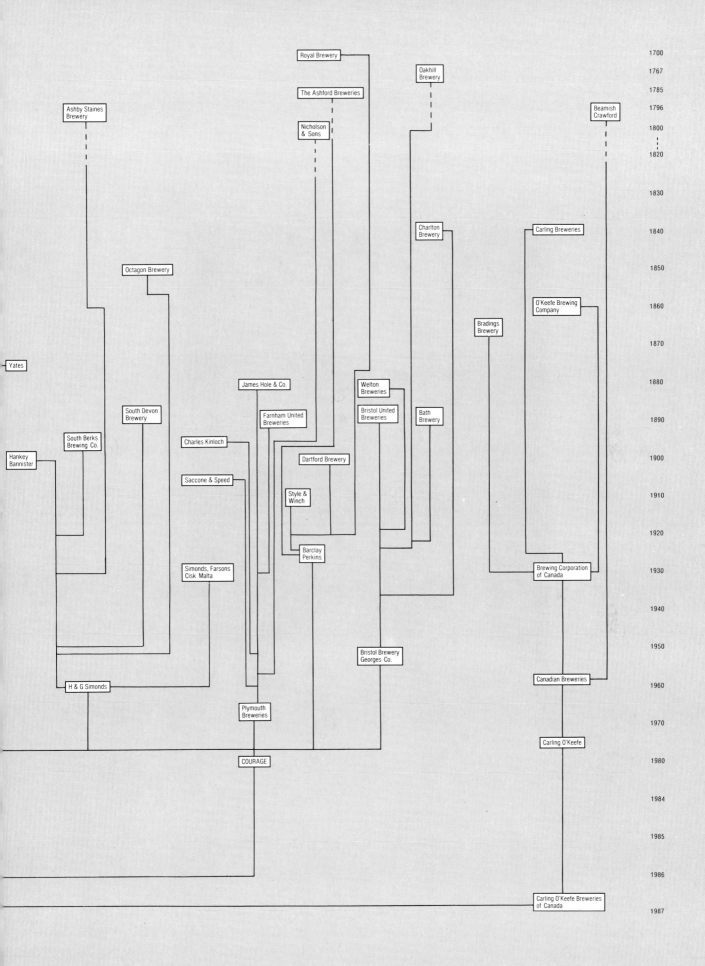

Royal Brewery

Oakhill Brewery

The Ashford Breweries

Beamish Crawford

Ashby Staines Brewery

Nicholson & Sons

1700
1767
1785
1796
1800
1820

1830

Charlton Brewery

Carling Breweries

1840

Octagon Brewery

1850

O'Keefe Brewing Company

1860

Bradings Brewery

1870

Yates

1880

James Hole & Co.

Welton Breweries

South Devon Brewery

Bath Brewery

1890

South Berks Brewing Co.

Charles Kinloch

Farnham United Breweries

Bristol United Breweries

1900

Hankey Bannister

Saccone & Speed

Dartford Brewery

1910

Style & Winch

1920

Barclay Perkins

Simonds, Farsons Cisk Malta

1930

Brewing Corporation of Canada

1940

Bristol Brewery Georges Co.

1950

H & G Simonds

Canadian Breweries

1960

Plymouth Breweries

1970

Carling O'Keefe

COURAGE

1980

1984

1985

1986

Carling O'Keefe Breweries of Canada

1987

Alexander Elder — launched the business on a hogshead of whisky and a puncheon of rum.

OVERTURE

From a Trickle to a Torrent

The port of Kirkcaldy is a bitter place to be in the darkling days of the Scottish mid-winter. But in the high summer of 1839, with sunbeams sparkling off the Firth of Forth to make the coats of the dray horses glisten, there was a magic about the place. Certainly there was excitement for George Elder, a successful merchant and shipowner, and his son Alexander Lang Elder on the afternoon of 15 July. They were on the quay to watch the crew of the 89-ton schooner *Minerva* (David Reid, master, plus a mate and three seamen)[1] stow the last of an important cargo. George Elder and his sons had decided on a bold adventure: they would extend their business to the fledgling colony established only three years earlier at Adelaide in South Australia. It was agreed that Alexander, then aged twenty-four, would lead the way, voyaging in the family-owned *Minerva* with a cargo of sixty barrels of tar, nine casks of biscuits, agricultural tools and nails, seeds, clothing and linen, gunpowder and six thousand roofing slates.[2] Among the last items to be manhandled aboard was one hogshead (in those days, 63 imperial gallons or 286 litres) of whisky, one hogshead of brandy and a puncheon (anything from 72 to 120 gallons) of Jamaica rum—and Alexander put two gallons of rum and two pounds of tobacco in his tiny cabin for his enjoyment on the voyage.

George Elder and his other sons, William, Thomas and George, jun., plus a good proportion of Kirkcaldy's 2,600 population[3] were on the quay the following day to wave farewell to Alexander when the *Minerva* sailed on the morning tide—just six men in not much more than a cockleshell embarking on a voyage of more than twenty thousand kilometres. They called at Cape Town and, after twenty-four weeks and two days, dropped anchor in the roadstead at 'Port Misery',[4] now Port Adelaide.

When Alexander put up his sign 'A. L. Elder, General and Commission Agent' and started his business by selling the cargo, you can be sure the spirits were in strong demand—although, if shared among the ten thousand or so colonists then in Adelaide,[5] there would hardly have been a dram per person. One hundred and fifty years on, that tiny family enterprise is today Elders IXL—an empire with revenues of more than $14 billion a year.[6] In grain trading, Elders Agribusiness challenges the five family giants who are at the centre of the world's food supply, the 'Merchants of Grain'.[7] In gold, oil, gas and coal, Elders Resources, which started from nothing in 1986, is now a $2 billion enterprise.[8] In the money market, Elders Finance has grown from the smallest merchant bank in Australia to the largest inside five years and operates internationally from fifty-four offices in fifteen countries.[9] And that trickle of spirits from Rundle Street has swelled into an ocean of Foster's lager, selling all over the world (although not yet at John Fisher's Harbour Bar at Kirkcaldy, where the whole thing started).[10] Elders Brewing Group is now the sixth biggest brewer in the world and will certainly get much bigger.[11]

The growth of such an empire can be likened to the mighty river systems of the world: the Mississippi, the Amazon, the Danube, the Zambesi, the Ganges. If one mentally imposes Elders on Australia's all-important Murray-Darling river system, one can visualise the original Elder Smith partnership formed at the headwaters of the Murray, to be joined by Commonwealth Wool at the Goulburn and Goldsbrough Mort at the Campaspe; Henry Jones IXL developed from the catchment of the Murrumbidgee; the Wood Hall group (including AML & F, among others) flowed down the Lachlan, and Carlton and United Breweries developed from the tributaries of the Darling. This corporate river system embraced much of the pastoral and agricultural history of Australia as well as much of our heritage in food and drink, and many of its streams sprang from mining and resource discoveries. In looking at the growth of Elders IXL, one observes a cross-section of the growth of Australia.

Each contributing flow was the result of the vision and energy of one man or a handful of men and the people they gathered around them: in the main Elders stream, the legendary Thomas Elder and Robert Barr Smith and Peter Waite, and also the auctioneers Thomas Sutcliffe Mort of Sydney and Richard Goldsbrough of Melbourne; in the Jones stream, Henry Jones himself, who put a waning Tasmania back on the map and made a further fortune out of tin mines in Thailand, and the patriarch Achalen Wooliscroft Palfreyman, who worked until he was ninety; in the Carlton and United stream, the brothers Foster, who quickly vanished back to America but whose name now goes round the world, and the formidable Cohen and Baillieu families. But, as with many of the rivers of this ancient land, the flow of energy in these corporate streams dwindled over the years. The companies wasted for want of vitality and verve. They found it in a quartet of bright beginners who, at the time the rejuvenation started, had an average age of just thirty.[12] John

Dorman Elliott was and is the leader; Richard Wiesener, Peter Damian Scanlon and Robert Maskew Cowper are his lieutenants. As corporate team players they attracted other bright young players to join them. Within little more than a decade, this team had brought all the streams together, breathed new life into them and loosed them upon the world—just as rivers, upon reaching their mouth, surge free into the sea.

John Elliott

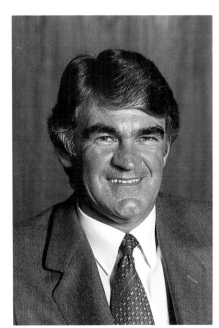

Peter Scanlon

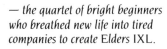

— the quartet of bright beginners who breathed new life into tired companies to create Elders IXL.

Richard Wiesener

Robert Cowper

The traditional — and now an ocean of Foster's selling around the world.

Sydney Opera House *by* **William Dobell** — *the flagship of the Elders Collection.*

PART ONE

Famous Foundations

chapter **1**

Building the
Elders Empire

The South Australia to which Alexander Elder made his way in 1839 was an unusual British outpost. First, it was the only colony in Australia to have no convict element whatsoever in its population; its men and women were there of their own free will. Secondly, it was the brainchild of the eccentric Edward Gibbon Wakefield, a Londoner who, while serving in the British embassy in Paris, eloped with teenage heiress Ellen Turner and was sentenced to three years in prison for his trouble. It was while he was in the notorious Newgate Gaol, sharing its crowded dungeons with convicts sentenced to transportation, that he developed the theory that such slave labour was not required for the founding of a colony and that free emigrants could make a success of it. He spelt out his ideas in A *Letter from Sydney*, published in 1829 while he was still behind bars.[1] In 1831 he was free but 'despised for his swinishness and coarseness'[2] when news reached London that Captain Charles Sturt had explored down the River Murray and across to Gulf St Vincent, covering promising farm land; so he influenced a campaign to colonise the new country, stressing the nub of his theory that settlers must buy their land and the revenue be used to promote the migration of ever more colonists. It became a popular cause and resulted in the House of Commons passing the South Australia Act in 1834, the act saying that no land could be sold for less than twelve shillings an acre (about forty dollars at 1988 values; see appendix).

The first colonists' ships anchored off Adelaide from July to December 1836, three years ahead of Elder. Even when the settlement was established, early arrivals had to overcome the problem of getting ashore from rowing boats. 'The shore is an uninhabitable swamp,' wrote one emigrant, 'and the few people who are living in the wigwams of Port Adelaide are too busily engaged in landing boards and rolling up casks to take any notice of a party of ladies and gentlemen up to their knees in mud trying to reach the shore. . . . Port Misery would be a better name; for nothing in any other part of the world can surpass it in every thing that is wretched and inconvenient.'[3] Few were dismayed, however, and Adelaide grew quickly. People built their homes and shops and stores to a town plan drawn by the estimable first surveyor-general, Colonel William Light, formerly Wellington's intelligence officer at Waterloo.[4] His plan for Adelaide, with its surrounding parks, and North Adelaide largely survives and makes Adelaide the most attractive city in Australia today.

By the time Elder arrived in the Minerva, Governor George Gawler had placed 4,400 people in the surrounding rural areas. 'Capitalist "squatters" ', wrote G. M. Trevelyan, 'introduced cattle and sheep farming on a large scale, and opened out an attractive field of enterprise for adventurous spirits.'[5] In his spare moments, Elder could enjoy Charles Dickens's Nicholas Nickleby, then being serialised in the South Australian Gazette. And 'when the governor and his lady, the civil and military officers, the clergy and most of the respectable inhabitants of Adelaide and the country districts gathered at Government House on the night of 28 December [1842] to mark the sixth anniversary of the foundation of the colony, they were brim full of joy.'[6]

Elder, having traded his first cargo, had a tough couple of years in Adelaide; but, with the Minerva plying regularly between Port Adelaide and Launceston, he managed to survive. And things picked up markedly when copper was discovered, first at Kapunda, seventy kilometres north-east of Adelaide, in 1842 and later at Burra, a further seventy-five kilometres north. Elder set himself up as a metal broker, and 'South Australia shot like a rocket into great and unexpected prosperity, taking the young Scotsman with it.'[7] He reported by letter to the family at Kirkcaldy a year later: 'Business matters keep in thriving condition here. . . . The mines have given our neighbours a high opinion of us, and last week 45 emigrants from Port Phillip arrived here per Hawk, principally miners.'

About this time Elder launched himself into pastoral pursuits, founding the firm's longest and strongest interest. He leased, in partnership with F. H. Dutton, the discoverer of copper at Kapunda, twenty thousand acres (eight thousand hectares) of marginal country near Mount Remarkable, in the Black Range of the Flinders Ranges, 225 kilometres north of Adelaide.[8] Squatting leases from the Crown in those days averaged a farthing an acre, or £20 16s ($1,250) for Elder's run for a year. But this Elder was really more urban minded, and when he was joined by his brothers William, a sea captain, in 1844 and George five years later, they concentrated on non-pastoral businesses: a gasworks in Adelaide, a guano fertiliser deposit beside Spencer Gulf, an iron smelter, and shipping. In addition to their own ships, they acted as agents for other owners, customs agents with bond stores, and even tendered for the transportation of convicts to Tasmania!

But life was not all work. Alexander married the daughter of a Congregational minister, the Reverend John Baptist Austin, and they had seven sons and five daughters.[9] He was a justice of the peace, a trustee of the Savings Bank of South Australia, a director of the Adelaide Auction Company and the treasurer of the local Church of Scotland; in 1851 he was elected to represent West Adelaide in the Legislative Council. He was, indeed, a leading citizen. But after thirteen years of colonial life he hankered for home; he resigned all his positions and left Adelaide, establishing his family a couple of years later in London, where for some thirty years he acted as agent for the company. He died in London in 1885, aged seventy. Brothers William and George left Adelaide soon after Alexander, both of them well off; William died in the south of France aged seventy-eight and George at Knock Castle in Ayrshire aged eighty-one.

That left the greatest Elder of them all to carry on and expand the business. Thomas Elder, the remaining brother, reached Adelaide in 1854 at the age of thirty-six. He was a bachelor and remained so. His sister Joanna—later 'Adelaide's most renowned hostess'[10]—was courted by one Robert Barr Smith, a son of the manse and a graduate of the University of Glasgow, who was then aged thirty-two.[11] About the time of the marriage, Thomas Elder set off in the company of three Legislative Councillors on a trip up the Murray River in the paddle-steamer

Robert Barr Smith — the careful, dutiful one of the Elder-Smith combination.

Thomas Elder — the greatest Elder of them all, who realised the potential of the outback.

Gundagai (Captain Francis Cadell, a pioneer of the Murray-Darling river trade, which was to be so important to isolated squatters); the purpose was 'to extend our knowledge of the capabilities of the Murray'.[12] They sailed from Goolwa, near the mouth of the Murray and some eighty kilometres south of Adelaide, at 8 a.m. on Sunday, 7 September 1856, heading across Lake Alexandrina, Elder noted: 'Considering the small sum charged for passage money from Goolwa to Albury, a distance of 2,000 miles, namely £15 [$850] including provisions, we had abundant reason to be satisfied with our fare and steward's attendance.' The following notes reveal some of the simple characteristics of the man:

> A whist party was organised and kept up during the voyage, but we never commenced till after tea, never played for money, and invariably ceased at ten o'clock. . . . During the day the changing scene and constant novelty was one continued feast. . . . Black swans and white cranes were also seen in great numbers. . . . As a means of amusement, we are frequently in the habit of lighting bonfires on shore after the vessel has moored for the night—the magnificent appearance of half-a-dozen bonfires within twenty yards of each other, the flames towering up to fifty or sixty feet in height and sometimes consuming whole trees under which the fuel has been placed, may well be imagined.

After crossing the colonial border of South Australia, and with New South Wales to port and Victoria to starboard, Elder noted, 'The natives here a much finer race of man than those in the vicinity of Adelaide. . . . Some appear—for the Australian Aboriginal, it must be remembered, is a very low species of humanity—pretty intelligent, but they wear very little clothing and have all the outward attributes of savages.'

Elder and a companion decided to do the last stage of the journey to Albury on horseback—and the Elders story very nearly came to an end right there, for in the uncleared bush they got lost:

> We had no provisions with us and didn't relish the idea of indefinite starvation. But there seemed no help for it, and my companion at last began to discuss with me the possibility of being compelled to slaughter a young foal which followed the mare he rode. . . . We providentially stumbled upon a log hut tenanted by a solitary shepherd who kindly directed us and, after considerable hardship, we reached Albury at midnight, where we found our friends waiting for us in the greatest anxiety—knowing as they did, from their own experience as bushmen, the perils we were exposed to.

Naturally the trip had business implications. Elder noted when the *Gundagai* was at Echuca, 'It is the nearest point on the river to the Bendigo diggings, from which it is only sixty-one miles distant, and the diggers are largely supplied with stores by the steamers.' In due course,

Elder branches at the river ports, such as Goolwa, Wentworth, Echuca and Wilcannia, and Bourke on the Darling, became 'established agents for river trade',[13] handling imports for the Victorian goldfields (on which South Australia levied customs tariffs, much to the chagrin of Victoria) and exports first of gold and later of thousands of bales of wool.

The brothers-in-law Elder and Smith had qualities that meshed well together; Elder was a visionary with a real feeling for the land, and Smith was a shrewd businessman and administrator; he later sat on more than a dozen boards, including those of the Adelaide Steamship Company and the AMP Society, and helped to found the Bank of Adelaide.[14] Their first formal association was in the partnership Elder, Stirling and Company, something of an interregnum in the march of Elders; the other partners were Edward Stirling, a considerable pastoralist whose name is scattered over maps of South Australia, and John Taylor, a businessman. This partnership lasted only six years, but it included one bonanza.

Walter Watson Hughes, a squatter and a retired sea captain, ran his sheep on a large lease at the head of the Yorke Peninsula, some 130 kilometres north-west of Adelaide. The Aboriginal name for the place was Wadlu Waru, meaning wallaby urine; Hughes shortened it first to Walla Waroo and later, because it was too long to stencil on a wool bale, to Wallaroo.[15] Hughes had a hobbyist's interest in geology and metallurgy, and he had been fascinated to observe that mallee roots tossed on a campfire burned with a greenish flame, so he had told his shepherds to be on the watch for possible minerals. One of them, James Boor, picked up on 17 December 1859 a green pebble which had been scratched up by a kangaroo rat while burrowing. He showed it to Hughes, who immediately registered claims in Adelaide and secured mineral leases. He also alerted the Elders partnership as to what was going on. Preliminary investigations suggested a rich lode of copper, and the Wallaroo Mining and Smelting Company was formed. But development work ran into serious trouble and the enterprise was shaky. Hughes approached Elders for an injection of £80,000 ($4.5 million) and got it, although 'great was the risk'.[16] The mine, worked largely by miners brought out from Cornwall, was a huge success, producing 10 per cent of copper to the tonne; the smelting works, built on the coast about five kilometres from the mine at what is now the town of Wallaroo, handled gold, silver, lead and tin as well as copper. Edward Stirling retired from the partnership on the proceeds, a very rich man.

But the best was yet to come. Paddy Ryan, another of Hughes's shepherds who was minding a flock about ten kilometres south of the original mine on country known as Moonta (Aboriginal for 'place of impenetrable scrub'), spotted more green pebbles at the entrance to a wombat's burrow, but either because he suspected its value or because he was known as a drinker whose word might not be taken seriously, he kept quiet about it. Then, inevitably, while drinking at the Port Wakefield Hotel, some forty kilometres from his hut, the booze got the better of him and he blabbed his news to the publican and a business-man named Mills.[17] While Mills headed straight away for Adelaide, an eavesdropper rode at speed to the Wallaroo homestead to alert Hughes. He dispatched his friend W. A. Horn and a companion towards Adelaide at once, urging them to beat Mills to the Land Titles Office to register claims blanketing the Moonta area.

At Port Wakefield, Horn learned that Mills had taken the direct coast route, so he took the longer inland route so that Mills would not be aware that the race was on. When still some sixty kilometres north of Adelaide, his companion dropped out exhausted. Horn secured a fresh horse and pressed on through the night. That horse broke down at the Torrens River. Horn ran to a stable and secured a third horse and galloped into Adelaide; he covered, in all, 264 kilometres in twenty-two hours.[18] When he and John Taylor, of the Elders partnership, entered the titles office at nine o'clock that June morning in 1861, Mills was there ahead of them. But the chief clerk was late; when he did hurry in he recognised Taylor and accepted the claims lodged by Horn on Hughes's behalf first.[19]

Mills's fury led to a select committee inquiry which reported against Hughes, who appealed to the Supreme Court of South Australia and won. The dispute was taken to the Privy Council in London but finally settled out of court; Hughes paid Mills and his associates 'several thou-sand pounds'.[20] That hardly mattered. For the Moonta mine was twice as rich as Wallaroo in copper and paid dividends of more than a million pounds. Hughes subsequently invested in huge pastoral spreads and was knighted for his public benefactions, which included a gift of £20,000 ($1.25 million) which helped to found the University of Adelaide.

John Taylor, like Edward Stirling, pocketed his copper fortune and left the partnership. This left Thomas Elder and Robert Barr Smith on their own, and on 31 January 1863 they launched the famous title Elder, Smith & Company. The draft agreement between them, in Elder's hand, is in the boxes of family papers in the Mortlock Library of South Australiana in Adelaide.

Cashed-up through copper, the partners—either together or with others—set out in earnest to acquire or lease huge tracts of pastoral land; by conservative count they at one time held 22,450 square kilometres—bigger by far than Wales or Northern Ireland and about one-third the area of their Scottish homeland! As surveys were rough in those days, they might indeed have had the use of land as extensive as Scotland.[21] Not for them the settled areas near Adelaide; they looked north, first to the Peterborough district on the way to Broken Hill

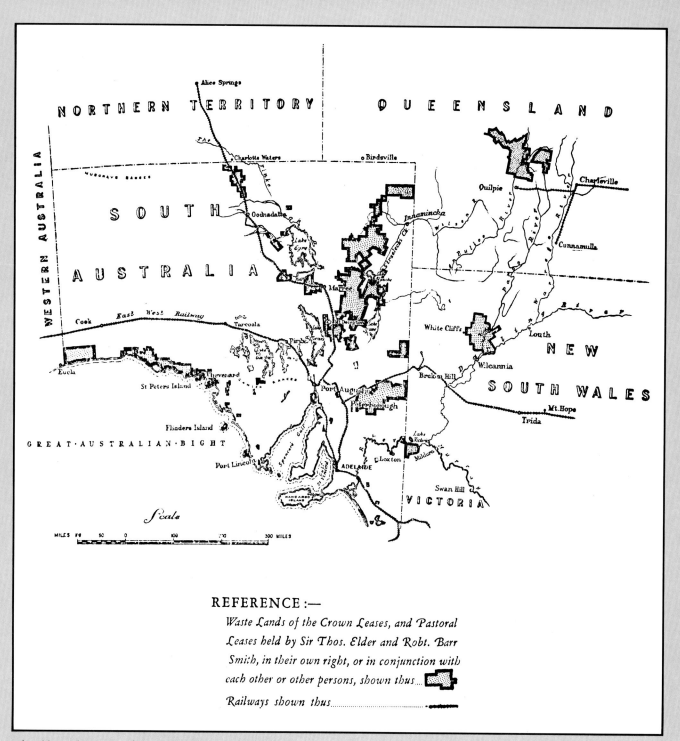

The Elder and Barr Smith pastoral
leases — from the Western
Australian border into Queensland.

(Paratoo and Pandappa—3,730 square kilometres between them), then to the lower slopes of the North Flinders Ranges (notably Beltana, of 2,300 square kilometres, and a string of properties astride the Birdsville Track, including Cordillo Downs in the north-east corner of South Australia, which juts into Queensland) and across the border to several big parcels of land in the Charleville-Quilpie-Warbreccan triangle. Robert Barr Smith also had a run of coastal properties from what is now Ceduna west across the Head of the Great Australian Bight to Eucla on the Western Australian border.

This was nearly all semi-arid country, and the risks were enormous, particularly from drought. An Elders company secretary testified to a royal commission later, 'Only men who had what has been described as very strong backbone have done any good in the outside country. . . . I have known men possessed of a few thousand pounds who have taken up outside country and have lost everything. Only men with very long purses are enabled to work that kind of country successfully.'[22]

Even at Paratoo and Pandappa, which were only 260 kilometres north-east of Adelaide, there was no surface water whatsoever. So Elder and his resident partner Peter Waite (another Kirkcaldy man, who later became chairman of Elder, Smith & Co.) were obliged to spend many thousands of pounds sinking artesian bores. The Great Artesian Basin, with an area of 1.75 million square kilometres, is the biggest such water store in the world; it made possible the settlement of vast tracts of South Australia, Queensland and New South Wales.[23] Stock and their owners still depend upon it today.

Elder and Waite were not only innovative with water; they also brought fencing to their huge runs. In one two-year period they imported 269 tonnes of wire from England to fence Paratoo's boundaries and divide it into great paddocks, at once getting rid of the shepherds with their huts and movable sheep pens and introducing the epitome of the outback, the boundary rider. This lifted the station's carrying capacity to 260,000 sheep.[24] When they opened up Beltana and Murnpeowie—much further north, just below the start of the Birdsville Track—they spent £214,000 ($7.3 million) over thirty years on water and fencing, but this allowed them to shear 363,000 sheep, a mighty flock.

Elder was full of good ideas. As a result of a trip to the Middle East when he was thirty-nine and on which he rode a camel from Cairo to Jerusalem in company with a party of Englishmen, he realised the value of camels to the outback.[25] So in 1865 he imported from what is now Pakistan 124 camels and thirty-one 'jemidars' to look after them.[26] The handlers became known throughout the outback as 'Afghans', although few of them had ever seen Afghanistan, and when the railhead was pushed up to Oodnadatta the train was known as the Ghan because

they were its keenest patrons.[27] Elder based his camels at Beltana, and an associate, N. E. Phillipson, reported, 'They were forthwith employed in transit of goods to various sheep and cattle stations, proving themselves to be of the greatest value as they were able to convey supplies during the most severe droughts. . . . The first great national work on which the Beltana camels were employed was in the construction of the Adelaide to Port Darwin (and London) telegraph line in 1872 when one hundred of them were made use of in carrying wire, insulators, provisions etc.'[28] Geoffrey Blainey has written, 'At one time half of the continent and its sparse, struggling population relied on pack camels.'[29]

Camels were used, too, in the expeditions of discovery wholly or partly financed by Elder in his desire to open up as much country as possible. The first saw John Ross, the manager on Umberatana (in 1870 the northernmost of Elder's stations, 720 kilometres from Adelaide), pressing north of Lake Eyre. It was clearly one of the rare seasons when

Elder's camels — 'Half of the continent and its sparse, struggling population relied on pack camels.'

the Channel Country in Queensland is awash and the Diamantina River and Cooper Creek fill the lake, for he reported to Peter Waite that there were '300 miles of river and lake in that region available for steam navigation'[30]—something of an illusion. In 1872–73 W. C. Gosse, using Elder camels but financed by the government, was astonished to find, some three hundred kilometres west of the telegraph line, 'one immense rock rising abruptly from the plain'.[31] It was, of course, Uluru; Gosse named it Ayers Rock after the South Australian premier of the day.

Elder and his mining associate Walter Watson Hughes in 1873 financed and dispatched an expedition from the telegraph station at Alice Springs led by Colonel Peter Warburton, the elderly commander of South Australia's volunteer army. His brief: to go due west until he reached the Indian Ocean, a distance as the crow flies of more than fifteen hundred kilometres, and to find some features to fill in the then-blank map. He set off through the spinifex with three European companions, an Aboriginal called Charlie, two Afghan drivers and seventeen camels.[32] After eighteen months on the track through parched desert, they eventually hit the Oakover River and followed it down to the tiny port of Roebourne, two hundred kilometres south-west of what is now Port Hedland. Only two camels survived, seven having been eaten so that the party could survive and the rest lost through misadventures. But without them the party would have perished.

Ernest Giles, having made a disastrous expedition using horses—during which he lost his companion Alfred Gibson, after whom the desert is named—set out again in 1875 with a string of camels from Beltana; his plan was to strike south-westerly in the hope of reaching the colony established at Perth. Despite having to cover, on one occasion, 520 kilometres without water, he made it, thanks to Elder's camels. He made it back, too, filling in more empty spaces on the map.

These expeditions showed clearly that there were few pastoral possibilities on the western side of the telegraph line, so Elder concentrated on the eastern side, stretching his leases up into Queensland. The Colonial Office recommended that townships should be established at Alice Springs, Charlotte Waters and Peake, a telegraph station not far from present-day Oodnadatta.[33]

Elder financed one more camel-carried expedition, in 1891 when he was seventy-three. It was, perhaps, the most intriguing. Called The Elder Scientific Exploration Expedition and launched on £5,000 ($350,000) of Elder's money with a promise of as much again if required, it was actually managed by the Royal Geographical Society of Australasia with a brief to fill in gaps on the map in central and western Australia.[34] The society selected as leader 35-year-old David Lindsay, South Australian born and an experienced surveyor and prospector and currently a sharebroker on the Adelaide Exchange—'a man of firm and decisive character'.[35] His party included nine other Europeans, four Afghans and forty-four camels from Elder's herds. Things went wrong from the beginning. Only five days after setting out from the railway line at Warrina—some one thousand kilometres north of Adelaide and eighty kilometres south of Oodnadatta—Bob Bowden, the man in charge of the camels, fell ill and died. Thereafter, they had to struggle through drought-stricken territory. The camels, 'notwithstanding that they were heavily laden, accomplished the extraordinary feat of 537 miles in 34 days without a drink';[36] the scientists resigned *en masse*, and, the proper area of exploration having been abandoned, the affair finished at the Murchison River, north of what is now Geraldton. Elder withdrew his support, and the expedition was disbanded.

The expedition had its repercussions. The scientists laid 'grave and serious charges' against Lindsay before the council of the Geographical Society; both sides were heard and Lindsay was exonerated, although the nature of the charges were kept secret. Elder concluded that 'the expedition had been beaten by the drought'. That version was accepted and echoed in a summary of South Australian exploration published by the Geographical Society in 1910.[37] But nearly a hundred years after the events, the lid was blown off by K. Peake-Jones—himself the author of the Geographical Society's commemorative book *The Branch Without a Tree*—in the twelfth Brock Memorial Lecture in Adelaide on 16 May 1985. Citing documents that had been either suppressed or edited beyond recognition at the time, he said that the claim that the expedition was 'one of the major achievements' was 'patently false. . . . The Expedition was a failure; less than a third of its allotted task was achieved; the party broke up in disarray; the leader was discredited.'[38] Peake-Jones revealed all sorts of things. First there was the doctor and the drink; Dr Frederick Elliott tried to take six cases of spirits with him. Lindsay sent four of them back. 'Lindsay did not like alcohol except for medicinal purposes; Elliott was its enthusiastic supporter both medicinally and socially.' Then Hadji Shah Mahomet, to whom responsibility for the camels passed, was very difficult. Lindsay recorded, 'The man was temporarily insane and had to be treated as a lunatic.' And many of the party were poor performers. Aubrey Gwynne, an English surveyor, 'could not be trusted to do any job properly', and Richard Helms, the naturalist, 'knocked him down'. All quite trivial, but in the middle of the never-never such 'personal incompatibilities' were devastating.[39]

Despite the Lindsay fiasco, Elder's contribution of camels was crucial to the development of the pastoral and mining industries in the outback. The movement of commercial camel trains was reported in the newspapers. 'Mr Acraman arrived from Port Augusta with 99 camels in charge of 45 Arabs and a Jemidar,' noted the *South Australian Advertiser* after the arrival of the camel train at Elder's Paratoo station;[40] its arrival twenty days later at his depot at Wilcannia, beside the Darling in western New South Wales, was also reported: 'The camels in charge of Mr Acraman and sixteen Arabs arrived—60 were laden with stores and merchandise brought across the boundary from South Australia.'[41]

On the pastoral side, it is safe to say that in the early 1880s Elder and Smith were shearing, on runs they owned or leased, at least 1.5 million sheep, yielding conservatively (given that fleece weights were lower then) thirty thousand bales of wool. At 1988 prices, such a clip would have grossed some $33 million.[42] But troubles lay ahead to decimate their flocks: rabbits and droughts. By 1887, the twenty-four rabbits imported on Christmas night 1859 by squatter Thomas Austin for sport on his property at Winchelsea in Victoria's Western District had so multiplied and spread throughout eastern Australia that the partners were obliged to employ 120 trappers on their two runs near Wilcannia. In six months they caught and scalped '618,000 rabbits on ground where probably not a rabbit lived only four years earlier'.[43] And the following year a frightful drought was upon the land, as Manning Clark has recorded in his distinctive style: 'The farther west a man went in 1888, the less belief he found in anything, the less hope for anything. The ancient continent was becoming as dry as the deserts in the hearts of its human inhabitants.'[44]

It was in that inauspicious year of drought that the partners offered shares in all their enterprises to the investing public. Elder, Smith & Co. was floated with an authorised capital of £1 million in £10 ($640) shares. The initial paid-up capital was £89,816 ($5.7 million), and total assets £437,584 ($28 million).[45] Thomas Elder and Robert Barr Smith each had 15 per cent of the issued shares, and Peter Waite just under 4 per cent; A. G. Downer, of another pioneering Adelaide family, had 9.6 per cent. Robert Barr Smith had been steadily building the company's financial and mercantile business as well as the shipping agency, particularly for the regular Peninsular & Oriental (P & O) mail steamers. Metal broking had prospered, too. But the core business was in wool, providing long-term finance to the pastoralists and, on the selling side, conducting auctions in Adelaide or arranging facilities for large-scale sales on consignment in London. (Originally nearly all Australian wool was sold on consignment overseas; only slowly did local selling develop, and even by the close of the nineteenth century Adelaide auctions accounted for less than 10 per cent of the Australian clip.)[46]

Thomas Elder did not sit on the board of the public company; he was seventy when it was established and preferred to spend most of his time in a baronial-style mansion, The Pinnacles, he had built on Mount Lofty, outside the city. He was already a respected senior citizen. He had served two stints in the Legislative Council for a total of thirteen years, sharing parliamentary duties with, among others, the Scottish-born miller John Darling, who was known as the Grain King because he was the biggest shipper of wheat from Australia.[47] (The name Darling occurs again much later in the Elders story.) Elder had been knighted in 1878 and promoted to Knight Grand Cross of the Order of St Michael and St George (GCMG) in 1887. For many years he raced horses but later concentrated on thoroughbred breeding at his Morphettville property (part of which is now Morphettville Racecourse). At his Blanchetown property he bred horses for the Indian army, a profitable business.[48] For the last ten or fifteen years of his life, his relationship with Robert Barr Smith was paternal on the one hand and filial on the other, although Barr Smith was only six years his junior. Barr Smith would write him three and four letters a day, reminding him of house guests, appointments, things to be done—or sometimes, as on 19 January 1889, very little: 'Dear Tom, nothing new to say.' He usually ended these notes 'Yours affectionately [or affctly], R. Barr Smith', but never Robert or Bob.[49] The nature of their relationship was illustrated startlingly in a note Barr Smith wrote to Elder about a forthcoming meeting of the Royal Geographical Society about the flawed Lindsay expedition, of which Smith was critical: 'I, of course, am willing to go to the meeting, and make any representations you tell me to make, altogether irrespective of my own views.'

It was from his Mount Lofty eyrie that Elder observed his company's most critical crisis. For the first four years as a public company, Elder, Smith & Co. paid its shareholders a steady 8 per cent; its results were:

Year	Net Profit	Paid Out in Dividend
1889	£8,487 ($543,000)	£5,000 ($320,000)
1890	£31,336 ($2 million)	£7,500 ($480,000)
1891	£21,408 ($1.5 million)	£9,000 ($630,000)
1892	£14,142 ($1 million)	£11,500 ($850,000)

But in 1893—'a year of unmitigated disaster', according to Sir Norman Young, a later chairman—profit vanished and the company reported a loss of £56,000 ($4.4 million). One source[50] says the directors were compelled to pass the dividend, while another[51] says they paid the shareholders £6,000 ($470,000). The accounts for the year showed provision for bad and doubtful debts of £78,982 ($6 million), some £60,000 ($4.7 million) of them among clients in the Western District of Victoria. Sir Norman Young says, 'They lost all their reserves; they were broke. Elders should have been wound up in 1893.'[52]

The crash occurred not only at Elders; it struck in every colony. But its impact was greatest in Melbourne where a mad property boom had raged like an epidemic for a decade. When the bust came, there was a run on the Melbourne banks and several of the apparently most solid closed their doors, ruining their depositors. Even the mighty W. L. Baillieu, the most brilliant businessman of his generation, was caught and was obliged to seek and get a composition with his creditors under which he paid sixpence in the pound (2.5 cents in the dollar) of his debts.[53] (The Baillieu name, too, plays a role later in the Elders story.) The impact on Elders was heightened by drought in the far north of South Australia, a drought that affected all of Australia for the following eight years—'the most severe in recorded Australian history'.[54] The national sheep flock was halved before good seasons returned. In fact, Elders recovered quickly and paid a dividend of 5 per cent in 1894 and a steady 6 per cent until the end of the century.[55] By 1896 the directors were spending £7,000 ($500,000) on the warehouses at Port Adelaide 'to meet increased wool selling business'.[56]

But time was running out for the great innovator; Thomas Elder died at The Pinnacles in 1897 in his eightieth year. In life and death he was a considerable philanthropist, specially to the University of Adelaide. In 1874 he matched his friend Walter Hughes's £20,000 ($1.25 million) to endow chairs in mathematics and general science; and over the next twenty-five years and in his will he added £31,000 ($2 million) for the medical school, £21,000 ($1.4 million) for the music school and £26,000 ($1.8 million) to general university funds. Somewhat surprisingly he gave £25,000 ($1.75 million) to the National Gallery of South Australia, for he had once complained that 'picture seeing is more fatiguing than people think'.[57] In final bequests he left £25,000 (nearly $2 million) for the founding of Working Men's Homes and £16,000 ($1.2 million) to hospitals and divided £18,000 ($1.3 million) among the Presbyterian, Anglican and Methodist churches. In 1988 values he gave away some $13 million in public benefactions. His total estate topped £800,000 ($60 million), built in just over forty-three years in South Australia.[58] Soon after his death, and under the leadership of his son-in-law Tom Elder Barr Smith, a fund was launched to finance a statue in Adelaide of the pioneer. His friends at the Geographical Society voted to donate ten guineas ($800) but considered 'it would be preferable to devote the fund now being raised to the erection of an Elder Science Hall, in which case the Society would be prepared to subscribe at least £1,000 |$76,000|'.[59] This good sense did not prevail, and the statue stands today.

Leadership of the company was now firmly in the hands of Robert Barr Smith, then aged seventy-three, as managing director, and Peter Waite, the pastoralist who preferred to spend his time on his northern properties, then aged sixty-three, as chairman. Though not young, they were still energetic. And as the twentieth century began, the seasons came good. Elders pushed into Western Australia in 1903 by forming a company with Sir George Shenton and others called Elder Shenton & Co. (which Elders took over entirely in 1918); this enabled them to be all-powerful in the wool business in South Australia and Western Australia for the next forty years.[60] Also in 1903, the company took over the firm of Livingston and Yates to establish a branch at Mount Gambier, in the state's south-east, and spent another £8,000 ($500,000) on 'additional wool stores and show floors at Port Adelaide'.[61]

In 1910, although he was eighty-six, Robert Barr Smith signalled that he was by no means finished. His 'financial acumen . . . and his counsel |were| largely responsible for the sound basis' on which Elder's Trustee and Executor Co. Ltd was launched;[62] within thirty years it had a capital of £90,000 ($3.6 million), reserves of £67,000 ($2.7 million) and trust funds of £14 million ($560 million). And three years later he expanded the company's important resources business by forming with others in Melbourne Elder's Metal and Mercantile Pty Ltd, buying out the others only a year later. But that was his last shot. He was into his nineties, and he died 'of senile decay' at his Adelaide home in 1915, leaving an estate sworn for probate at £1,799,500 ($93.5 million), 'the largest in South Australia until then'.[63] Like his long-time partner Elder, he left large amounts to charities and supported the university; he put up the money to complete the spires of St Peter's Cathedral, and, perhaps oddly, in 1908 he paid off the £2,300 ($160,000) debt on the Trades Hall. He also shared Elder's interest in racing, but not his taste for honours—Barr Smith refused a knighthood.[64]

The changing of the old guard was completed with the death of Peter Waite. He had been the founding chairman for thirty-three years and retired only months before he died in 1922. His estate was a much more modest £160,000 ($6.4 million). But his own generosity created his own memorial: the Waite Agricultural Research Institute. He provided the land for it—his fifty-four-hectare Urrbrae estate, plus forty-one adjoining hectares in what is now the south-eastern suburb of Mitcham—and he endowed its future by the gift of a substantial parcel of Elder, Smith shares.[65]

Tom Elder Barr Smith took over as chairman in the decade following World War I, which saw the company expand most handsomely: paid-up capital of £600,000 ($26.5 million) in 1918 was lifted to £2,050,320 ($82 million) in 1928; total assets rose from £3.4 million ($133 million) in 1918 to £5.6 million ($226.5 million) in 1928, and net profits more than doubled from £112,102 ($4.5 million) in 1918 to £252,346 ($10 million) in 1928—and dividends paid to shareholders ranged from 10 to 12.5 per cent a year. The company operated branches in all the capital wool-selling centres, and in the rural areas many former agencies were upgraded to branches.[66]

The ten fat years were, in modified biblical fashion, followed by ten lean years—the Great Depression of 1930–34 and the years of uncertainty leading up to World War II. Profits hit their nadir of £99,820 ($4.4 million) in 1931, and in no year before World War II did they equal the profits of 1928; dividends paid dropped to 4 per cent in 1931 and did not rise above 7 per cent. T. E. Barr Smith's report as chairman in 1930 reads ominously like speeches heard in Australia in recent years: 'There are many troubles in Australia today of the people's own making. As a community we have been over-borrowing and over-spending. . . . We must live within our national income and everyone must join in the sacrifices.'[67]

Elders weathered the lean years better than many companies, and an earlier history of the firm, *The First Hundred Years*, gives much of the credit for this to Walter Young, who became managing director in 1929: 'Of all the great personalities associated with Elder, Smith & Co. throughout its history, none surpasses Sir Walter Young in the greatness of services to the State.'[68] Young, born in the bush, joined the company when he was fifteen and worked his way up, becoming general manager at thirty-seven and managing director at fifty-seven—not young by 1980s standards, but much younger than Elders were accustomed to. His namesake, Sir Norman Young, argues that he represented a fundamental change in the company in which control by owners was replaced by managers: 'He was the first in a new line of professional managers who, during succeeding years, would claim and be granted very much wider powers in relation to the conduct and management of the Elders business.'[69] To be sure, many of Walter Young's tactics had to be defensive, but he went on the attack in 1937, taking over the wool firm of George Hague & Co. in Geelong, the second auction centre in Victoria after Melbourne.

The centenary of Alexander Elder's first enterprise in Adelaide coincided with the outbreak of World War II, when the highly competitive wool-selling business was put into government-controlled abeyance. Some solid landmarks had been established: Elders had principal offices in Adelaide, Perth, Melbourne, Sydney, Brisbane, Geelong and London; it had thirty-eight country branches in South Australia, twenty-five in Western Australia and two (Broken Hill and Wentworth) in New South Wales; it was agent for a dozen shipping companies, including P & O, and a ship charterer in its own right; it looked after six airlines, and it was either Australian or South Australian agent for more than eighty manufacturers, most of whom made things the farmers and pastoralists wanted; its banking business for rural clients was significant with £3,854,959 ($155 million) out to them in one form or another. Not a bad century.[70]

World War II saw the auction system for wool abandoned for the duration, the British government acquiring the entire Australian clip—for £60.9 million ($2 billion) in 1941, £73.5 million ($2.3 billion) in 1943, and so on, the money being distributed to the growers. Elders handled about 8.5 per cent of the clip right through the war.[71] The return to the open auction system in September 1946 saw the start of a dramatic five-year run in national wool revenues. The first full peace year was 29 per cent higher than the last war year; the second was up another 64 per cent, the third another 27 per cent, the fourth another 38 per cent and the fifth an incredible 125 per cent. This was the 1950–51 pinnacle, when wool requirements for soldiers in Korea—who fought in winter temperatures of 30 degrees below zero and lower—pushed prices through the roof. Graziers rejoiced at getting 'a pound a pound' for their wool. The national clip made £651.9 million ($12.3 billion), nearly nine times the revenue from the last war year and, indeed, the highest price wool has ever been.[72]

The competition to handle the biggest piece of the action was, naturally, intense among the wool brokers. The carve-up in 1947–48 was: 1, Dalgety with 14.5 per cent; 2, Goldsbrough Mort with 10.9 per cent; 3, Elder Smith with 10.1 per cent; 4, New Zealand Loan and Mercantile with 8.2 per cent; 5, Winchcombe Carson with 7.0 per cent. The top five handled together more than half of all the wool sold. The desire to increase market share unleashed more than thirty years of takeovers, even though total revenue was more than halved in 1951–52 and has never, not even now, regained the height of the golden year.[73]

Elders started its campaign as cautiously as one might expect with a leader who had been chairman for more than twenty-five years. The company consolidated its strengths in South Australia by taking over De Garis & Sons, who were strong agents in the south-east and slightly across the Victorian border, for £200,000 ($6 million), and in Western Australia by buying Paterson & Co., who were traders in machinery and fruit as well as agents, for £65,000 ($1.7 million); and it made a nibble into Victoria by acquiring the interests in that state of Commonwealth Wool, a Sydney-based wool broker and station agent, in 1950.[74] This lifted the number of Elders branches to 116—51 more than just before World War II—but still the concentration was in the south and west with only fourteen in the Western District of Victoria and still just two in far-western New South Wales. But then, during the summer of 1951–52, a new general reported into headquarters at Elder House in Currie Street, Adelaide. He was Henry Norman Giles, the company's next truly charismatic leader. During the next twenty-four years he was to expand Elders enormously. It is also true to say that he established such a one-man reign and such a bureaucratic style of management that the shift of Elders power base from Adelaide to Melbourne became inevitable.

Giles was born in the Perth suburb of Claremont, the son of the local livestock manager for Elder, Smith. He attended Christ Church Grammar School (indeed, he later rescued the school's finances), where he was given the nickname Skinny—a name that stuck, even though he grew into a commanding figure of a man. His schooling was cut short by the death of his father, and the fourteen-year-old started working in the stockyards. 'Elders men were born and bred in the stockyards,' a former executive commented. 'The company culture was that if you didn't wear elastic-sided boots and if you didn't know how to sell sheep and cattle in the yards, you had no qualifications.'[75] Qualified or not, Giles did well and climbed the ladder to become manager in Perth before he was forty.

He was summoned to Adelaide as second-in-charge to Lachie Sanderson, the managing director—'a wonderful chap, but incompetent'.[76] Within two years Giles was managing director! Well aware of his own failure to complete an accountancy course (but not entirely naive about money, as his share-market speculation, which started when he was at school, made him a millionaire),[77] he called in a top man whom he had met during his Perth days: Norman Young. Six years Giles's junior, Young was born in Glasgow but went to school and university in Adelaide and set up in practice as a chartered accountant, specialising in taxation (although he published his first book when he was thirty-one on *Bankruptcy Practice in Australia*). 'It was my role,' Young recalls, 'to call on my clients, who were managing directors; to chat, and to drink Scotch.' During an early chat, Giles mentioned a company tax

Norman 'Skinny' Giles — 'Elders men were born and bred in stockyards.'

ruling which Young considered to be wrong in law; he pursued it, and the Taxation Commissioner was obliged to send the company a cheque for some £75,000 ($1.2 million)! The directors did not need much urging by Giles to invite Young to fill a casual vacancy on the board despite Young's 'inability to produce an acceptable social pedigree'.[78]

Skinny Giles recognised that market share in the wool-broking business was largely a matter of territory. He was aware that the purchase of George Hague & Co. just before World War II had seen Elders' share of broking in the important wool port of Geelong, where competition was fierce, rise from 17.5 per cent to better than 21 per cent inside ten years.[79] So he wasted no time in acquiring the New South Wales operations of Commonwealth Wool and Produce; the total price for those and the earlier-purchased Victorian branches was £1.1 million ($16.3 million). He also grabbed the Newcastle broker and agent New England and Northwestern Producers (NENCO) for £796,000 ($11.8 million) to complete fairly good branch coverage of New South Wales. And he extended into Queensland by buying the solid firm of Morehead Limited—founded in the 1870s by Boyd Dunlop Morehead, a politician as well as a businessman who once held thirteen stations in the Mitchell district—for £587,000 ($8.7 million).[80] Thus, by the 1956–57 wool-selling season, Giles had rearranged the broking totem pole. Elder, Smith sat on the top with 15.4 per cent of the national clip, an ascendancy it has never surrendered; Dalgety was second with 14.8 per cent, Goldsbrough Mort third with 11.8 per cent, New Zealand Loan & Mercantile fourth with 9.4 per cent, and Winchcombe Carson fifth with 7.3 per cent.[81] It meant too that the company was active in all states except Tasmania and conducted wool auctions in all seven major selling centres: Adelaide, Melbourne, Sydney, Brisbane, Perth, Geelong and Newcastle.

It was a splendid start for the new chief executive. Not that he kept his fellow directors well informed. Sir Norman Young recalls:

> The directors had never seen, nor asked for, an operating or capital expenditure budget; they had never seen, nor asked for, a monthly profit and loss statement, and they had never seen, nor asked for, a positive long-term program that might be expected to diversify the company's operations and make it less dependent upon uncontrollable wool, sheep and cattle prices. . . . They spent most of their time at board meetings poring over lists of advances made to customers and offering comments, often based on favourable or unfavourable social judgements, as to the financial creditability of the debtors.[82]

To be fair, Giles did ask Young to establish proper methods of financial control and reporting, which he did with Charles Faggotter, 'a man endowed with a most acute accounting brain'[83] (and currently the company secretary of Elders IXL).

Giles, although deeply into the saleyard culture, could see other fields. The company bought 40 per cent of the real estate financier and developer Lensworth Finance (and finished buying it in 1979), took a substantial parcel of shares in Commercial Union Insurance when it was floated in Australia, and joint-ventured with the Chase Manhattan Bank and others in Esperance Land and Development, bringing into production 445,000 hectares of virgin land in Western Australia.

Going into the 1960s, Elders had improved its share of the nation's wool broking to 16.44 per cent; its assets were worth more than £20 million ($250 million); its liabilities were about £12 million ($154 million), and its disclosed capital and reserves about £8 million ($102 million). 'The company also had considerable "secret" reserves which had been largely created on the recommendation of Norman Giles.'[84] The next two years were to see the two mightiest mergers in Australian pastoral history. They were brought about by two main factors. First, the value of total Australian wool production—on which the brokers seek to make their selling commission—took a dive in the late 1950s from £507 million ($7 billion) in 1956–57 to £363 million ($5 billion) in 1957–58 and £311 million ($4.3 billion) in 1958–59, a fall of 39 per cent over three seasons.[85] Secondly, inflation and costs—particularly the costs of ever-bigger warehouses and show floors—were rising sharply. 'The directors and executives of wool-broking firms discussed these questions among themselves without finding much cause for optimism.'[86] Their worries were enhanced by the credit squeeze of 1960.

The first of the big bangs was the marriage of the two biggest British-owned houses, Dalgety and the New Zealand Loan and Mercantile Agency, late in 1961. Both had long histories. F. G. Dalgety had arrived in Sydney in 1833, several years ahead of Alexander Elder, and after a confusing array of associations launched Dalgety & Co., financed by English investors, in Melbourne in 1884. New Zealand Loan and Mercantile was launched in London in 1864 to invest in properties and trade in produce in New Zealand, extending operations to Melbourne and Victoria in 1874.[87] Both had weathered the crash of 1893 and the Great Depression of the 1930s, and as late as 1948 NZL & M had taken over Schute Bell Badgery Lumby Ltd, brokers and agents strong in Sydney and Newcastle, for £263,000 ($6.8 million).[88] But the bank crackdown, which virtually trebled the demand on pastoral houses for advances to wool growers, forced NZL & M to seek a merger. In fact it was a takeover, the new firm being called first Dalgety and New Zealand Loan Ltd and later simply Dalgety Australia. (Of interest in that takeover is the fact that John Madden Baillieu, grand-nephew of the great W. L. Baillieu, was a director of NZL & M and moved onto the new Dalgety board to serve for many years before switching, for reasons which will emerge, to the board of Elders).[89]

The Dalgety takeover was observed, of course, by Norman Giles;

Thomas Sutcliffe Mort — he established the first regular wool auctions in Australia.

Richard Goldsbrough — a Yorkshireman with a liking for the good life.

observed, too, by the directors of another famous pastoral house, Goldsbrough Mort & Co. Ltd, which was third on the broking totem pole behind only Dalgety and Elders. The Goldsbrough Mort combination might be called the Peace of the Roses, for Richard Goldsbrough sported the white rose of the Yorkists and Thomas Sutcliffe Mort the red rose of the Lancastrians.

Mort was the first to arrive in Australia, in Sydney in 1838, from Manchester in Lancashire, his father's death four years earlier having robbed him of a comfortable start in life. He was determined to repair his fortunes in the colony. And he did. Five years after his arrival, he set himself up as an auctioneer, and although he was not the first to auction wool in Australia, he did establish the first regular wool-only sales. In 1855 he established Mort & Co. to both auction and consign wool and, soon after, to provide pastoral financing; his biographer says he provided 'an integrated set of services to pastoralists that formed the pattern for later wool-broking firms'.[90]

Goldsbrough, who completed a seven-year apprenticeship in Bradford, the wool capital of Yorkshire, ran a successful business for five years, sorting and packaging wool to manufacturers' requirements, before sailing for Melbourne. He arrived in 1847 and again classed and packaged wool for growers and merchants and also classed sheep on properties. He, too, established regular wool auctions, the first in Victoria. And he began speculating in properties, including Perricoota, Ballingerambil and Tatallia in the Riverina and Traralgon West in Gippsland. By providing credit for pastoralists he was able to do very well out of the squatting boom in the 1860s. He made a bid for Mort & Co. in 1882 and, when that failed, opened his own branch office in Sydney; this led to the amalgamation of Goldsbrough Mort & Co. in 1888. While Mort was an entrepreneur who put money into ship repairs, heavy engineering and early refrigeration, Goldsbrough put much of his great energies into the good life. He was a big and boisterous Yorkshireman, given to singing and laughing and eating and drinking; an inventory of his cellar after he died included 150 gallons of whisky, nearly as much brandy and sherry, and thirty-six gallons of port which had been in the bottle for more than sixty years! He enjoyed many a lady, too, and his heir, Richard Goldsbrough, was born to him by the wife of the brother of one of his partners.[91]

Goldsbrough Mort had to suspend dividend payments in the crash of 1893,[92] but the firm survived and grew in the 1920s, buying out Sydney rivals Harrison Jones Devlin Ltd and expanding into Elders' territory in South Australia and the west by taking over Bagot Shakes and Lewis Ltd. (John Lewis, the founder of that firm, was the father of Essington Lewis, a later chairman of BHP; this purchase launched a long relationship between Goldsbrough Mort and the Big Australian.)[93] The push into Western Australia was advanced by the purchase of Henry

Wills & Co. of Perth. Again in the later 1940s after the end of World War II, Goldsbrough Mort took over the Brisbane wool broker Fenwick and Co. and swallowed yet another wool-selling rival in Sydney, the Australian Wool Brokers and Produce Co.[94]

In the wake of the Dalgety–NZL & M marriage, Norman Giles opened talks with Goldsbrough Mort's general manager, Geoffrey Wyatt Docker, who had worked his way up through the firm over nearly forty years. The 20,000-plus shareholders (11,150 in Elders and 9,050 in GM)[95] were informed shortly afterwards that discussions had begun 'regarding the possibility of co-ordinating the operations and development' of the two companies.[96] In less than six weeks the deal was done. The chairman of Elders, Sir Philip McBride (a minister in Menzies' administrations both before and after World War II and then the federal president of the Liberal Party) and the chairman of Goldsbrough Mort, C.Y. (later Sir Colin) Syme (who was then chairman of BHP, a director of several companies and president of the Walter and Eliza Hall Institute of Medical Research) announced jointly 'a holding company to be called Elder Smith Goldsbrough Mort Limited, with a nominal capital of £25,000,000 [$315 million] divided into 50,000,000 shares of 10/- [$6.30] each'.[97] It was all very amicable. 'Business was conducted within certain rules of good behaviour,' Sir Norman Young said recently. 'There is no good behaviour any longer.'[98]

In fact it was another triumph for Norman Giles. The new corporate headquarters was in Adelaide; for that reason, among others, Colin Syme declined the invitation to be the chairman (although he stayed on the board), which let in Giles's man, McBride. Most of the board were Elders men. And by 1964, only two years later, of the fifty-eight executives listed in the annual report, forty-three were Elders men (74 per cent) and only fifteen former Goldsbrough men.[99] Certainly the shareholders were smiling. The merger announcement had forecast that the new company would 'be able to maintain a dividend at the rate of 8 per cent', but it was 10 per cent for the years 1964–66, 11 per cent for 1967 and 1968 and 12 per cent for 1969 on net profits which rose from £1,800,678 ($22.3 million) in 1963 through the currency change from pounds to dollars in 1966 to $6.03 million ($31.3 million) in 1969.[100] And in the fifth selling season after the marriage, Elders GM handled 28.06 per cent of the clip delivered into brokers' stores—a mighty 1,371,500 bales—and was leading Dalgety by 313,300 bales, or 30.75 per cent.[101]

By now Giles was at the height of his power, dominating his ageing chairman and most of the board. 'He gave them hell,' recalled a former executive[102]. His nickname of Skinny had assumed a new meaning; he was obsessed by keeping down costs, and he kept his eyes on them by being on every subsidiary board. 'He would get down to the very smallest detail. For example, if Doggett [Doggett Aviation & Engineer-

Sir Norman Young — from Glasgow to the better board rooms of establishment Adelaide.

Elders solid Adelaide headquarters — dwarfed now by the bank building.

ing, a crop-dusting, partially owned subsidiary, later liquidated] needed a new propeller costing a thousand dollars, they would have to get board approval, and he was there.'[103] And he was mean with salaries. 'They were always regarded as a cost, not as a factor in earning money.'[104] A former stud stock officer with the company recalls, 'A stockman working for Australian Mercantile Land and Finance in the yards at Hay was paid more than the branch manager of Elders . . . and Elders was totally bureaucratic.'[105] Sir Norman Young sums up: 'Salaries in Elders were appalling. I have lived a life of discomfort by being associated with a philosophy perpetuated by a chief executive and later chairman, representing the owners, to the effect that there are ''workers and us''. It was applied maliciously, so that the clerks and typists in head office were rewarded and protected while the workers—the branch managers, the people in the wool stores, the people who worked on the production lines—got very little. They had no superannuation, no fringe benefits; they were just bloody workers, just making the profits.'

Giles, aware that he would become chairman (in 1967), had much earlier chosen his successor as chief executive in the hope that he could develop him in such a way that he (Giles) could effectively retain direct power.[106] Harold Charles Schmidt, a man of impressive carriage and phenomenal memory, left Maryborough Technical College in Victoria quite early to work first on the railways, sometimes as an engine driver, and then in a private agent's business trading in sheep and cattle at Deniliquin, New South Wales. Elders bought out the agency. 'Giles saw Schmidt performing in the yards and said to himself, ''I like that bloke; he will be my successor.'' And so he was. But the plan backfired because Schmidt took over.'[107]

Giles was not one-eyed in his interest in pastoral business. He did diversify; under his chairmanship, Elders invested significantly in the Gove Alumina and Robe River mining ventures—and got caught for $150,000 when Mineral Securities went down in the crash that followed the Poseidon nickel boom.[108] Elders Finance & Investment Co., based on skills acquired in the early years of the unofficial, short-term money market, was launched as a merchant bank in 1970, and Elders Metals Ltd in 1971.[109] But Giles and Schmidt always watched for ways to expand their wool broking and in 1971 acquired the Victorian business of Younghusband Ltd, founded by William Younghusband, who had been a major investor in the River Murray Navigation Co. with Francis Cadell, the skipper on Thomas Elder's river trip so many years earlier.[110] Younghusband handled about 3 per cent of the national wool clip. Among Giles's final deals were a majority investment in the 4.1 million one-dollar shares issued to establish Beef City, a high-quality feedlot near Toowoomba in Queensland, and the purchase of the old-established wool-buying firm of John Sanderson & Co. for $199,125 ($.6 million).[111] Giles's long innings ended in 1975 after nearly fifty-four years with Elders, more than twenty of them as the commanding figure. Even though he retired as chairman, he left his stamp and style on the company.

The new team of Young and Schmidt gave shareholders a long-overdue boost, lifting after-tax profit in the next five years· by nearly 200 per cent, from $8 million ($20.8 million) in 1976 to $23 million ($36.8 million) in 1980.[112] They kept going after broking share, too; they bought Pitt, Son & Badgery in 1976 for $3.7 million ($9.7 million). This was a famous old firm, founded in 1879 by George Matcham Pitt and his son with Henry Septimus Badgery, which successfully advocated the erection of saleyards at Homebush for the supply of meat to Sydney. Pitt, who in his young days had explored and then settled the Gwydir River district of northern New South Wales, was said to have a voice like thunder and liked to cap his arguments with quotations from Robert Burns.[113] For years Pitt, Son & Badgery had a little over 3 per cent of the national wool-broking business, and in 1977 it helped to lift Elders' share of all wool sold by 3.65 per cent to 34.59 per cent, a huge 1.2 million bales which grossed $326 million ($848 million).[114]

The company, however, was set concrete-hard in its ways. When a girl ledger machinist collapsed in the heat of the monolithic Currie Street office and a young clerk suggested to the director of administration that something had to be done about ventilation (in the days before air-conditioning), he was told, 'You have to go through the correct channels.'[115] The same clerk, rather more senior in 1980, put up a proposal which would eliminate much of the repetitive typing and save time and money; after months of delay he was told by the general manager, administration, 'We've decided not to approve your idea. We'll look at it again in a couple of years.' It was, of course, a word processor![116] No, life in Elders moved with the tranquil speed of the seasons. The directors (but not Young, who is no clubman) lunched with grazier clients at the Adelaide Club, and executives met less-exalted clients at the excellent Chesser Cellars—and there was not much work done after lunch.[117] Young wrote later, 'We were, perhaps, no longer an attractive target for a take-over bid.'[118] He was wrong.

chapter 2
The Extraordinary 'Jam Tin Jones'

Within thirty years of its settlement, Tasmania was recognised as a splendid place to grow things. 'Every fruit, vegetable and flower that thrives in England, thrives better in Van Diemen's Land—especially apples, peaches and plums; but gooseberries, currants, raspberries and strawberries also attain great perfection. . . . Nectarines, apricots, grapes, figs, mulberries, water and mush melons are met with in many gardens. . . . Walnuts, filberts and almonds have been raised in many places.'[1] No wonder that the earliest manufacturing in Hobart included jam making,[2] and that jam making—and many other enterprises besides—was to be dominated by one Henry Jones; so much so that the Left later talked of 'Henry Jones' Jam Monopoly'.[3]

The blood in Henry Jones's veins was as Welsh as 'Land of Our Fathers'. Jack and Emma Jones sailed from Wales as free migrants and tried farming in the Green Ponds district before settling in Hobart, where Jack worked as a counting-house clerk. Henry, their first child, was born on 19 July 1862 in their home opposite the Wesleyan chapel in Melville Street.[4] Emma, a devout soul who had the Welsh regard for learning, sent him to Mr Canaway's School—later the Hobart Central School—for an elementary education. As these were still the days of child labour, she found him a job when he was twelve, in a somewhat unusual factory.[5]

George Peacock was an eccentric. A Somerset man, he migrated to Hobart and established a successful fruit and grocery retailing business and married the widow Margaret Pryde. Observing that his customers had a liking for jam, he opened one of Hobart's first jam factories and by 1870 operated in splendid stone premises in Hunter Street opposite the Old Wharf (now Victoria Dock). When Henry Jones reported for work in 1874 he found that before anything else was done Peacock

Henry Jones — from sticking on labels to owning an empire.

'read prayers to his employees and, after exhortations, the short service ended with a hymn suitable to the occasion and season. . . . Rough behaviour and swearing were not permitted in the factory; blasphemy earned a serious lecture; signs of alcohol drinking, dismissal.'[6] Henry's first job was sticking labels on tins of jam for twelve hours a day, earning four shillings ($12) a week plus threepence (75 cents) an hour for overtime.

The ambitious Henry realised he needed more education. For three years he attended the Hobart Town Night School (later the Hobart Technical School), where he was a top student, excelling in commercial subjects, mental arithmetic and general knowledge.[7] At much the same time he learned a lesson in life, as he related later: 'One night I had been drinking in the Ocean Child Hotel and I came out and could not walk home. I sat down on the curbstone and felt dreadful. I said to myself: "Henry Jones, you've lost the use of your legs, and soon it will be your head and your good job. I'll never be anything if I keep drinking, and I want to be an important man in business." I decided then never to touch alcohol until I was in an important position, and I not only kept my resolution but I've never drunk any alcohol since.'[8]

He was promoted to jam maker—it was boiled in great copper pots—and when he was still under twenty-one he married 'a striking auburn-haired, handsome, well-built young woman, physically and mentally capable in every way for the strenuous life of the wife of a thrusting, restless, most ambitious man'.[9] Alice Glover bore him a dozen children, nine daughters and three sons, all of whom survived to adulthood. When he was twenty-three, Henry was made factory manager. That same year, the staff was joined by an eleven-year-old who was to have almost as much influence as Henry himself: Achalen Wooliscroft Palfreyman. He travelled from his home in Launceston to answer an advertisement for an office boy, and he was interviewed by old man Peacock, who asked him if he could play the organ. 'I said I could—mother had seen that every boy and girl could play—and Mr Peacock took me to a large room in his factory where there was an organ. "Play such-and-such a hymn," he said, and I did. He began singing the hymn and asked me to play a couple more. Then he asked me if I could sing. I said I could, in a fashion. We sang a duet—*Onward Christian Soldiers*, I think it was—and I was offered the job at two shillings [$6] a week. . . . The organ playing was probably decisive.'[10] A year later Palfreyman sought a rise in pay and received this note from Peacock: 'What you want is not an increase in salary, but an increase in gratitude. Get down on your knees three times daily and give thanks that you have constant work and that your employer pays you each week.'[11]

While Jones and Palfreyman did indeed have steady jobs, the business was in deep trouble; the boiling and canning machinery was ageing, and the peculiarities of intercolonial trade were crippling. Federation was still more than a decade away, and so was the Constitution of the Commonwealth, with its all-important section 92: 'trade, commerce, and intercourse among the States, whether by means of internal carriage or ocean navigation, shall be absolutely free.'[12] Before the late 1880s, when income tax was introduced progressively, the separate colonies depended upon tariffs to pay for much of their public works and civil servants. Victoria, egged on aggressively by David Syme of the *Age*, had the heaviest protection: from 1852 a tariff on all incoming spirits, wines, tobacco, tea, sugar and coffee, from 1871 a sliding 10 to 20 per cent tariff on all foreign or intercolonial imports, and from 1877 even on livestock—owners moving cattle and horses from New South Wales and South Australia had to pay five shillings ($16) a head and ninepence ($2.40) on every sheep.[13] Even New South Wales, which bragged about its free-trade philosophy, used the 10 to 20 per cent sliding scale of tariffs for a while.[14] These tariffs hit Tasmanian jams, which had become popular in all five mainland colonies. A device to avoid them was to parboil the fruit and ship what was called 'pulp', which did not attract a tariff, and finish the boiling in the colony of destination. Peacock had opened a factory in Sydney for this purpose. Even so, he fell foul of the colonial secretary, George Dibbs, an ardent protectionist, who accused him in the Legislative Assembly in Sydney of bulking his jams with pumpkin, squash and rotten fruit with only enough actual fruit pulp to give the flavour.[15] A further allegation that a tin of Peacock jam had poisoned a family of six in Sydney did not help.

By 1889, when he was sixty-five, George Peacock had had enough and retired to the Sydney suburb of Petersham to sing his hymns and say his prayers—and forget the business which was, to all intents and purposes, bankrupt. Rescue operations in Hobart were mounted by the three-man partnership of Henry Jones, Achalen Palfreyman and Ernest A. Peacock, one of George's eleven children. Each put in £500 ($32,000); Henry's nest-egg had been saved by his practical wife during the first six years of their marriage, Palfreyman's came from his father, and Peacock had family money.[16] Their £1,500 ($96,000) was not enough, so Jones turned to a former team-mate of their younger days in the Railway Football Club (one of the three teams in the Hobart Australian Rules competition), David Barclay, who had become manager of the Commercial Bank of Tasmania. The bank backed the partnership.

The 1890s were not easy years to try to rebuild a business. The property boom of the 1880s had gone bust, banks were closing their doors (the Van Diemen's Land Bank crashed, but the Commercial Bank survived), and unemployment was acute throughout Australia. But Jones, the managing partner, moved to a home near the factory and got stuck into modernising the plant. He also adopted the brand IXL for his jams and canned fruits. Asked to explain, he said, 'I *excel* in all the products I make. It is my motto.'[17] By 1898 he had extended the premises opposite the Old Wharf and installed seventeen new, large copper boilers to make jam, which led *The Cyclopedia of Tasmania* to describe the works as 'the leading business of its kind in Tasmania, if not in all the Australian colonies'.[18] He was canning apricots, plums and tomatoes as well as making raspberry, strawberry and gooseberry jams and tomato sauce, consuming 544 tonnes of fruit a season, which filled two million cans, all made on the premises—hence his nickname 'Jam Tin Jones', which, following his knighthood some twenty years later, became 'Knight of the Jam Tin'.[19]

In addition, Jones had established a branch factory on-site beside the fruit at Franklin in the Huon Valley, forty-five kilometres south-west of Hobart, so that he could boil the raspberries in their prime. Previously the berries taken in barrels by sea to Hobart had tended to ferment and

Selling jam — the Palfreyman method.

result in inferior jam. He also went into the export of fruit and hops: in 1898 he shipped sixty-five thousand cases of 'green fruit', mostly apples, to London; he was 'among the largest exporters of hops'; and he sold canned fruits to Africa, India and 'other parts of the East'.[20]

Life was not all toil. He was a generous patron of the newly formed North Hobart Football Club (and, no doubt, his 150 full-time employees and 350 seasonal workers barracked for the team), the Hobart Amateur Athletic Club and, of all things, the Homing Pigeon Society. But he showed no interest in the Hobart Hunt, the Hobart Polo Club or horse racing, all of which flourished at the time. His personal relaxation was a game of billiards with such friends as His Honour Norman K. Ewing, headmaster Leonard Linden of Hutchins School and later Warden of Christ College, and sawmiller Henry Gray.[21]

In October 1899 the first contingent of Australian troops embarked for South Africa and the Boer War, to fight, not for the last time, Britain's battles. Over the next three years, 16,175 officers and men left Australia; 518 did not come back.[22] They were good years for jam makers, for there was the new demand for the taste of raspberries and strawberries to relieve the boredom of a military ration made up largely of bully beef and biscuits. Henry Jones did well, not only out of army and navy contracts but through expansion. In 1900 he and Palfreyman had gone to Sydney to buy and amalgamate the Sydney Jam Company and Boyce Brothers to become H. Jones & Co. (Sydney). Palfreyman stayed on for a while to bed down the operations. And in 1902, again with Palfreyman on hand, the OK Jam Co. of Melbourne—launched originally by William, another of George Peacock's sons—was

Henry Jones' original sign.

purchased and turned into the Australasian Jam Company (AJC).[23]

Henry Jones, aged forty and in his business prime, had made big plans; structural changes for further expansion were called for. The Jones-Palfreyman-Peacock partnership was dissolved and replaced in 1903 by the public float of H. Jones and Co. on the Hobart Stock Exchange with initial capital of £72,000 ($5 million). This was soon lifted to £350,000 ($25 million), because Federation, which put an end to the intercolonial tariff war and ushered in free trade between states, gave rise to vastly increased business.[24]

A diversion, which was to make Jones as much money as all his other enterprises put together, arose when his good friend Ted Miles, thirteen years his senior, returned from one of his many trips abroad. Edward Thomas Miles, the son of a Hobart cobbler, had played many roles. He went to sea at fourteen as a ship's boy and within ten years had his master's ticket, trading in the South China Sea and Gulf of Siam. By now a dapper figure with a spade beard and a sharp brain, he had returned to Tasmania to deal in ships and charters and then to enter, and do well in, the coastal trade, taking over his rivals and eventually selling out at a fine profit to the Union Steamship Co. of New Zealand. He put his money into property and developed railways and harbour breakwaters. He was elected to the House of Assembly and became minister for lands and works in the Braddon government in 1899 but was obliged to resign within months because a select committee found that he had behaved dishonestly, improperly and secretly in the matter of break-water tenders. The resultant motion of no confidence brought down the Braddon government. Not dismayed, Miles ran for and won the seat of Hobart the following year, but, such was the outcry, he resigned for the second time after only six weeks. Perhaps discretion prompted him to go back to Asia, to deal in ships, to contract to pave the streets of Manila with wooden blocks, to sell sleepers to the Indian railways.

On his travels, Miles visited the out-of-the-way port of Tongkah on the island of Phuket, near the south-western tip of Thailand (then called Siam), and observed that Chinese miners were using most primitive dredging methods to recover tin-bearing sands from the harbour bed. He knew something about dredging from ventures in northern Tasmania, and he recognised that Tongkah could be a very good thing. He hurried back to Hobart to drum up investment support, getting it from an enthusiastic Henry Jones, among others. The IXL Dredging Syndicate was formed to advance the project. Miles secured a concession to mine, promising in return to build a deep-water dock and dredge a shipping channel.

The Tongkah Harbour Tin Dredging Company was floated in Hobart in 1906 with Jones and Palfreyman as principal investors. Miles designed a bucket dredge which was assembled at Penang, on the Malay Peninsula, and towed by the steamer *Padang*, under his command, across 320 kilometres of the open Andaman Sea to Tongkah. It was put into successful and rich operation, establishing tin as Siam's third biggest export earner after rice and rubber throughout the first half of this century.[25] In 1919, for example, Tongkah paid dividends of £517,500 ($22 million). (The company remained on the Hobart board until 7 July 1982, when it was delisted at the directors' request because the number of shareholders had dropped below listing requirements.[26] Captain Miles died in Melbourne in 1944, aged ninety-five, leaving an estate valued for probate at £27,976 [$900,000].)[27]

Meanwhile, back at the jam factory, Jones took onto his board two newcomers: Alfred Ashbolt, a New Zealander who also became rich through Tongkah, and George Edwards, a former football team-mate who gave up a newspaper career to go into the new federal House of Representatives and was an expert on tariffs and the emerging Commonwealth Court of Concilliation and Arbitration, which was transforming industrial relations.[28] Together they boosted the company's timber activities (packing cases for fruit were vital) and shipping operations as owners and agents, and advised on Jones's personal investments in Tasmanian hydro-electricity and zinc extraction.

Across Bass Strait, Palfreyman became permanently based at the Australasian Jam Company in Garden Street, South Yarra. He followed the acquisition trail, buying the Red Heart Jam Factory in Carlton, the Rising Sun Jam Company and the Studley Preserving Company, and in 1907 he added the Geelong and Western District Preserving Company.[29]

Henry Jones's vision was not limited to Australia. He made a reconnaissance through South Africa and selected Rayden's Limited of Upper Paarl, some seventy-five kilometres outside Cape Town. He did a deal with its founder, J. S. C. Rayden, in 1905 to take a piece of his fruit and vegetable processing and canning and ultimately control; some years later he paid Rayden a 'special bonus' of £3,000 ($120,000) in full settlement of any goodwill attached to his name in connection with the labels, etc., used by the company'.[30] Over the long haul, South Africa was to prove the best food-industry move Jones ever made. As London was crucial to his export business, he sent a Hobart businessman, F. W. Moore, there to reconnoitre. This led to the establishment of F. W. Moore and Company, with authorised capital of £10,000 ($650,000), to act as London agent for all the Henry Jones operations as well as for Tongkah tin.[31]

It was a characteristic of Jones's acquisitions—he by then manufactured in four states and one overseas country—that each show ran itself without too much central control. But the early years of Federation had written new rules, particularly concerning wage-fixing and protection against imports, although imperial preference gave easier entry to goods made in Britain—and the City of London still had huge investments in Australia. On the advice of his director (and tame MP) George Edwards, Jones and Palfreyman, then his deputy chairman, decided that a holding company was required for the group. Accordingly, Henry Jones Co-operative Limited was listed in Melbourne in 1909 with a nominal capital of £500,000 ($34 million). It had almost no staff and was more of an 'investment company—maintaining the share register, paying dividends, filing tax returns and preparing a consolidated balance sheet from those produced by each of its subsidiaries. . . . Decisions were often transmitted to subsidiaries on Australasian Jam Company letterhead.'[32]

The new structure signalled new activities. Money was put into Cunliff and Paterson Ltd, which made jam and canned fruits in Melbourne under the management of Lancelot James Watson, and Abel Hoadley's sauces, pickles and vinegar business in South Melbourne was financed; both were later taken over completely and amalgamated.[33] There was public criticism of monopoly; but a Hobart academic, Professor Herbert Heaton, talked of a 'horizontal monopoly' which did not result in policies harmful to the public.[34] (Half a century later, communist adherents were still playing the same record: 'The coming of Federation in 1901 opened the way for a few of the larger |jam| factories of Hobart and Victoria to amalgamate and eliminate their rivals. . . . Henry Jones wields great power over fruit growers of Tasmania. It is the shipping agent for most of the produce going in and out of the port of Hobart.')[35] Jones said at the time, 'We are not here to exploit our suppliers or purchasers of goods, and we don't want to take away anyone's business from him. We have plenty enough ourselves.'[36]

Personally, Jones moved into a splendid new house and garden in Campbell Street, Hobart, with plenty of room for his growing family and a large billiard room for happy evenings with his friends. He also planned his first voyage abroad. In 1911, in his fiftieth year, he went with his wife, Alice, to the United States, Ireland, England and, of course, Wales. No doubt he heard Irving Berlin's 'Alexander's Ragtime Band', the rage in America that year, and at Covent Garden he might well have enjoyed an early performance of Richard Strauss's Der Rosenkavalier; certainly he witnessed all the pomp and pageantry of the British Empire in the coronation of King George V, and he was handsomely entertained in the City of London.[37]

He was back in America inside two years, keen to expand into California. He went to San Francisco with Palfreyman, and they toured the rich San Joaquin Valley, famous for its vegetables and both wine and table grapes. They picked Oakland, at the head of the valley and directly across San Francisco Bay from the Golden Gate Bridge, as their centre for operations—but all plans had to be put on hold.[38]

World War I saw the introduction of government controls over the production and marketing of commodities, the birth of pooling arrangements, acquisition committees, control boards, and so on; it also saw the launch of many fruit-growing co-operatives. Jones was called upon for his advice, and he became heavily involved as honorary adviser to the British government, guiding the realisation of substantial British investments in Tasmania to raise money to pay for food and military supplies from Australia and New Zealand. In the Victory Honours after the war, George V made him a Knight Bachelor 'for good and faithful services to Ourselves and the Empire'.[39] In a cheery wartime episode, the mayor of Hobart, William Williams, sought to boost war funding with something quite new to staid Hobart: a Carnival Queen competition. Six of the seven entrants raised financial support for their cause from special-interest groups, but the seventh, Jones's unmarried daughter Millicent, ran as the Citizens' Queen. The Hobart *Mercury* reported: 'With pomp and ceremony befitting the occasion, the Citizens' Queen, Miss Millie Jones, was crowned Queen of the Carnival at the City Hall. . . . It was a brilliant spectacle, doubtless unique in the City of Hobart, and the climax of a movement which will long be remembered as the means of raising the wonderful sum, approaching £10,000 [$500,000], for the benefit of those brave lads who are fighting the battles of Empire.'[40]

Jones, having worked with Prime Minister Billy Hughes to secure scarce post-war shipping to lift Tasmania's apple crop to Britain, wasted no time in getting back to California. He bought a factory in Oakland and planned to start operations with the opening of the fruit season there in May 1920. His aim was to complement jams shipped to the North American market from Australia, making in California 'only the varieties—having regard to the heavy duty and freight—which cannot profitably be manufactured on this side'.[41] The scheme did not flourish, probably because the Oakland plant was dependent upon American can makers and simply could not get enough of them to make the project workable. In a rare failure, Jones abandoned the enterprise after four years.[42]

A thrust into New Zealand was more successful. He bought into, and later bought out, an Auckland firm, Thompson and Hills (R. F. Thompson and F. M. Hills), which preserved fruit under the Oak label, and a Nelson outfit, S. Kirkpatrick & Co. Ltd (C. Milner and W. F. Thomson), jam makers and fruit and vegetable canners under the K label. As he had so often done in Australia, he left the management in local hands.[43]

A measure of Jones's standing in the business community and life of Hobart came in an incident with Tasmanian Labor leader J. H. Lyons, who was later to switch political sides and become a conservative prime minister of Australia. Manning Clark has recorded it: 'It was perhaps a hint of things to come that when asked to form a Labor Government [in Tasmania] in 1923, he [Lyons] sought advice from Sir Henry Jones,

Chairman of IXL, the "knight of the jam tin", rather than from his colleagues in the Labor Party.'[44]

But by now this entrepreneur, who had been a workaholic for more than half a century, came under a physical cloud: heart trouble. He had the energy and determination, however, to travel to his plant in Keswick, in suburban Adelaide, to sort out a strike—'one of the few, perhaps only, strikes experienced by the Jones group'[45]—which the press in 1923 said stemmed from piece-work payments and insanitary conditions; he got his people back to work. In the spring of 1926 he travelled by train from Hobart to Launceston and then aboard a Bass Strait ferry to Melbourne to forward negotiations for a British tyre manufacturer, Lionel Rapson, to open a plant in northern Tasmania. He attended a meeting on the morning of 29 October and repaired to his hotel for lunch. After his meal he did not feel well and decided to rest in the lounge. A heart attack killed him at 5.30 p.m. He was sixty-four. He left an estate valued at £112,646 ($4 million).[46]

More than ten thousand people—one in every five of the population of Hobart at that time—spread across the cemetery at Cornelian Bay in a last salute to Tasmania's greatest businessman. Their numbers were swelled, no doubt, by fruitgrowers from the nearby valleys, whose local paper eulogised:

> He repeatedly saved the small fruits industry from disaster by his exceptional skill in finding new markets and organising the trade. The exportation of enormous quantities of apples overseas from this State was also made possible in the early days of the business through his capacity to handle transactions on a big scale. He was known personally to more citizens of Tasmania than any other person and few, if any, could be found to speak ill of any transaction they had with him. . . . A name that will be honoured by Tasmanians for its integrity for generations to come.[47]

The death of Sir Henry Jones left A. W. Palfreyman in charge. He was just fifty and keen to expand. The years between the world wars were not easy; the growth of growers' co-operatives, many of them subsidised, challenged existing businesses in the 1920s, and the Great Depression flattened sales in the 1930s. But Palfreyman both launched new enterprises and took over existing ones. Dorothy Morgan, who researched the extensive but chaotic Jones papers at the University of Melbourne while preparing a thesis and has followed through the company's annual reports, has distilled the deals on a state-by-state basis:

> Victoria: On the growing side, financed and then acquired the Murrumbah Orchards, with 300 acres of pear trees in the Goulburn Valley; formed the Tatura Cultivation Co. to grow figs (and later asparagus near Warragul in Gippsland); planted the Horsham Cultivation Co. to peaches, and took over Panleek Brothers, hop and

tobacco growers at Eurobin, near Myrtleford in the Ovens Valley, extending tobacco growing to Ferny Dale in Tasmania and Rostrevor in South Australia. On the manufacturing side, took control of the Bendigo Preserving Co. and Wonderland Fruit Products of Richmond. And in timber, took over Bentley Downie's case-making mill at Toolangi, near Healesville; took over Tasmanian Hardwoods which was incorporated in Victoria, and took over the Pioneer Woodware Co. with a case-making mill in the Lilydale–Yarra Glen district—this firm made wooden clothes pegs as well as providing AJC with cases.

New South Wales: Consolidated manufacturing operations in Sydney, putting Oakleaf and P.J.C. under the banner of H. Jones & Co. (Sydney) and took over a case-making mill at Kendall, near Port Macquarie, as part of IXL Timber.

Queensland: After years of nibbling, Palfreyman moved formally in 1929 by taking over Victoria Cross Manufacturing, a jam and sauce maker and a fruit canner which had been owned by the Duthie family for thirty years and had acquired the condiment maker J. E. Burnard along the way. At the same time, Palfreyman took over the State Cannery, started by the Queensland government after World War I to handle pineapples grown by soldier settlers. A decade later the two companies entered a joint venture with a growers' Committee of Directors of Fruit Marketing (COD) known as Queensland Canneries which eventually handled 80 per cent of the State's pineapples.

South Australia: No aggression here, but operations continued through the Keswick plant which was noted for particularly good apricot jam, most of which went for export.

Western Australia: Not much action here either, although in the 1930s D. J. McKenzie Pty Ltd was taken over to distribute IXL and AJC products.

In South Africa the fruit and vegetable processing at Paarl was expanded by the acquisition of Western Province Preserving Co. and in 1937 a further new factory was opened in Johannesburg—a move which was to prove important as World War II approached.[48]

The war saw a complete government clamp-down on exports, not least because Australia became the base for huge American forces after the Japanese attacked Pearl Harbor, in Hawaii, in December 1941. That export ban opened the way for the South African factories to boost their shipments to Britain and win an enduring slice of the market.

An illustration of Palfreyman's innate shrewdness came after the fall of the Malay Peninsula and Singapore to the Japanese early in 1942 (with thousands of Australian diggers being taken into cruel and deathly jungle imprisonment). The price of shares in tin mines in Malaya—and at Tongkah—plummeted to pennies, and Palfreyman was one of the few buyers. Producing a swag of such share certificates years later, he explained, 'If the Japanese had won the war and occupied Australia, they would have undoubtedly shot me. But if they lost the war, the tin shares had to be valuable. So I was a consistent buyer.'[49] He cashed in for millions after the war.

Bureaucratic controls continued for several years after World War II; building permits for expansion were particularly difficult. Palfreyman was in his seventies, yet he clung to corporate power, grooming no successor. (His lifestyle was remarkable: round his home in Toorak, where real estate values had been astronomical since the land-booming 1880s, house cows grazed, surely the last farm animals to be paddocked within five kilometres of the Melbourne GPO.) The annual reports show that the company was in a shrinking mode for the first twenty years after the war; several factories, including Wonderland in Melbourne, were wound up, and in Queensland the firm grip on pineapples fell apart, leaving the company with only 25 per cent of the crop. Only in South Africa did things move forward, probably because the executives were spared from interference because of distance. New factories were opened at Port Elizabeth in 1949; at Malelane in the Transvaal, where they turned tomatoes into sauce, paste and puree, in 1954; and at East London, where they handled pineapples and grapefruit, in 1957.[50] In fact, by the early 1960s South Africa was the company's strongest profit centre.

Year after year the company paid a 10 per cent dividend, usually covered about three times by the declared profit. Commenting on this, the financial editor (anonymous in those days) of the Melbourne *Age* wrote:

> A necessary condition of the abstemious dividend policy has been Mr Palfreyman's own large shareholding in Henry Jones; this reduced the takeover risks that such a margin of undistributed profits would involve for most companies. . . . For a long time now, Mr Palfreyman has been a millionaire. Besides his great holding in Henry Jones, he was considered the biggest personal shareholder in BHP. . . . Mr Palfreyman's family was also found to be the biggest holder in Huddart Parker (steamships) when Boral made its takeover approach. And it was with Mr Palfreyman that Ready Mixed Concrete had to negotiate when it wanted to take over Consolidated Tin for its rich liquid assets.[51]

It was not until his ninetieth birthday, in January 1965, that Palfreyman agreed to resign. He had held the sole right to veto for forty years—and there is no recorded evidence that any of his fellow directors objected. As he prepared at long last to step down, he told a reporter from the *Sun News-Pictorial*, in his first and last newspaper interview, 'It would be presumptuous of a man of my age to make long-range plans.' But he admitted that he would like to watch some more of his horses—raced in the ownership of 'A. Wooliscroft', his given names—in the winner's enclosure. His horse Defence, the last son of the mighty Carbine, had won the Australia Cup many years earlier.[52]

The fact was that, for many years past, his dead hand at the helm had undone much of the entrepreneurial success of Henry Jones. A company employing some fifteen thousand people in nearly forty subsidiaries had gone to sleep. Palfreyman's inheritors of responsibility, most of them elderly, did take a few positive steps. They no doubt fulfilled an unrecorded wish of the founder by changing the name of the holding company from Henry Jones Co-operative to Henry Jones IXL. They extended manufacture to Western Australia by taking over H. Rayner and Sons, a family-owned jam maker and canner, so as to acquire management to run the new factory they built at Manjimup, in the fertile area about two hundred kilometres south of Perth. And, surprisingly, they bought into the new and totally unrelated business of commercial television, the initiative apparently coming from Sydney, where executives had bought fruit from growers in the Murrumbidgee Irrigation Area for years; in association with other MIA business groups they invested in Murrumbidgee Television, located at Griffith.[53]

But the reputation for being 'the most conservative company in Australia' still stuck,[54] and its leaders did earn the condemnation that followed their ultimate downfall: 'The intertia of the Palfreyman years turned to doddering stagnation after his death. Board members and many of the senior executives were in their late 70s and were not about to change what had supported them quite comfortably for the past half century.'[55]

chapter **3**
The Beer Barons Unite

The brothers Foster, who gave their name to the beer whose name is recognised from the Falklands to the Faroes, are as flashing phantoms in recorded history. Cyril Pearl, who wrote *Beer, Glorious Beer* twenty years ago, could do no better than 'the Foster brothers who came from New York'.[1]—puny obeisance to two men who revolutionised Australian drinking. Keith Dunstan, the latest praise-singer in *The Amber Nectar*, did much better. He identified them as W. M. and R. R. Foster, who arrived in Melbourne from New York in 1886, built their brewery and—after a stay of not more than three years—sold out 'far too quickly a lager that was destined to be famous even in their own country'.[2] But even Dunstan, a terrier for historical facts, could not give them their given names or their ages or their exact movements, even though he searched every likely archive in Australia and America. (My own searches of passenger lists of the period in the Public Records Office also failed to answer those questions.)

The Fosters are important because they stood brewing in this country on its head. The established method was known as top fermentation, in which the yeast rises to the surface of the brew. It was the traditional English method of making ale—flat, heavy, dark, warm and, above else, sweet. But the Fosters followed the German method of bottom fermentation, in which the yeast sinks to the bottom and in cooler, slower circumstances results in a lighter, longer drink, which must be served cold. In a word, lager. It had been tried before. The Germans Renne and Friedrich opened their Gambrinus Brewery in Melbourne in 1885, 'specially fitted up and devoted solely to the production of lager beer',[3] but within two years had gone down the tube with debts of £4,637 18s 8d ($325,000).[4] The Cohn brothers of Bendigo, who survived for generations in the soft-drink business, gave it a try in their Excelsior Lager Beer Factory, also in 1885.[5] The Fosters were the first to make a success of it, although they were not confident enough to hang in personally.

CARLTON BREWERY, MELBOURNE.

The original — the imposing Carlton Brewery in Melbourne.

The facts appear to have been as follows, based heavily on Keith Dunstan. The Fosters sailed into Melbourne in 1886, bringing with them a German-American brewer called Sieber who had studied in Germany, a refrigeration engineer called Frank A. Rider, and all the specialised equipment they required. They established the Foster Lager Brewing Company and built a brewery on an acre of land in Rokeby Street, Collingwood, for £48,000 ($3.4 million). The *Australian Brewers' Journal*, which for years had campaigned for 'a lighter, less intoxicating, more gaseous and better-conditioned ale than is brewed at present', enthused at the time, 'It far excels any brewery that we have seen in Australasia.' Brewing operations were started in November 1888 and the lager was held for at least sixty days at a low 35 degrees Fahrenheit (just under 2 degrees Celsius).[6]

It should be noted that these were wildly prosperous days in Melbourne. The land boom of the 1880s was at its height; indeed, it is quite likely that word of the boom was what beckoned the Fosters to try their luck in Australia. While their brewery was abuilding, some 270 new

The most famous poster — 'I allus has wan at eleven.'

companies with paid-up capital totalling £25 million ($1.75 billion) were registered in Melbourne, and properties in Swanston and Elizabeth streets rocketed from £400 ($28,000) to £1,100 ($77,000) per foot of frontage.[7] As nearly ten kilometres of pipe to carry the cooling brine were put in place at Foster's, the domed Exhibition Building just a few blocks to the west rang with speeches at a series of occasions to mark the centenary of white settlement, and 'the dresses of the barbers' wives and the pawnbrokers' wives caused the ladies of Toorak and the Government House circle to snort with disgust'.[8]

Early in the morning of the first day of February 1889, the horse-drawn lorries rolled out of Foster's brewery laden with crates of bottled lager, the corks secured with wire. The lorries carried something else new, too: great blocks of ice, which were given free to the publicans so that they would serve Foster's as it should be, ice cold. Dunstan has reported that 'Foster's was an immediate hit'. In the hottest month of the year, the drinkers of Melbourne rejoiced in a brew so cold, so refreshing. But when the chilly winds of winter blew, business was not so good.

The importers of lagers from Germany and the United States determined to stamp out this local upstart by dropping their prices from eleven shillings ($38) and twelve shillings ($42) a case to seven shillings and sixpence ($26) a case. The Foster brothers were obliged to appeal to the colonial government for protection in the form of an increased tariff on imported lagers. They succeeded, and the tax was raised from one shilling and sixpence ($5.25) a dozen to three shillings ($10.50), for Victoria believed in protection while New South Wales boasted of its free-trade philosophy. But during the debate, one MP who was also a rival—G. Downes Carter, chairman of the Carlton Brewery and an imposing figure with white mane and beard—revealed to the House that the Fosters had been trying to sell off their brewery for months. And he was right. As soon as the tariff was raised, they found a buyer; and just forty-one weeks after making their first deliveries, the Fosters sold. They remained in Melbourne just long enough to hand over the business and collect their cheque for £45,440 16s 10d ($3.2 million), which represented a considerable loss. Then they sailed away, as unheralded in their departure as they were on arrival. No other account of them survives, not so much as a snapshot.[9] Only the name—what a name! —lives on.

The new directors were again a fairly anonymous trio: Alfred D. Hart, Turner and Thomson. But the brain behind them and the man whose office they used for their early board meetings was altogether outstanding: Montague Cohen. The son of a salesman, Cohen grew up in Collingwood, read law at the University of Melbourne, and was good at cricket and football as well as being a keen cross-country runner—he later founded the Amateur Sports Club of Victoria and became president of the Victorian Amateur Athletic Association. While working as an articled clerk, he launched and ran a literary and debating society, one of whose best speakers was Alfred Deakin, later to become three times prime minister of Australia. When he was only thirty, Cohen became a founding partner in the law firm of Pavey, Wilson and Cohen—Pavey's—and quickly built a reputation for his business as well as his legal astuteness.[10]

The Foster Lager Brewing Company was still quite small beer! Production in the first month of new ownership, December 1889, was only some seventeen thousand bottles a week. They were having trouble with the ice-making machine, and as boom turned to bust and banks

Foster's first — always served icy cold.

started closing their doors, the Bank of Australasia was twitchy about the overdraft of £33,000 ($2.3 million). But the actual beer was excellent, and the early 1890s saw a couple of good breaks. In 1892 the Victorian government imposed an excise of threepence ($1) a gallon on all beers made with sugar—which included all the English-style, top-fermented brands—but only twopence (66 cents) a gallon on beers produced from pure malt and hops and with no sugar; this gave bottom-fermented Foster's a strong sales boost. Then in 1894, Monty Cohen, who had joined the board, recruited the remarkable Auguste Joseph Francois de Bavay as chief brewer.[11]

De Bavay was a man of considerable parts. Born into an ancient

Belgian family (genealogy back to 1193), he graduated first as a surveyor and then as a chemist and brewer—and later as a bacteriologist and metallurgist—and did research work in Europe, making contact with, among others, Louis Pasteur. But in his mid-twenties, frustrated academically and financially, he went to Ceylon as a tea planter. In 1884, when he was twenty-eight, he was engaged by the veteran brewer Thomas Aitken to become the chief brewer at Victoria Brewery in Victoria Parade, East Melbourne. He embarked on solid research into the wild yeasts of the day which caused second and third fermentations, ruining the beer. Within four years he had developed a pure yeast, which was the first used commercially in Australia, and a year later produced Melbourne No. 1, which became the basic yeast in Australian brewing. At the same time, in his role as a bacteriologist, he won first attention and then acclaim for revealing that the fire hydrants in the streets of Melbourne were lethal in that they were the conduits for sewage, with a heavy load of typhoid and diphtheria, to enter the water supply. A royal commission found that he was right. Then, when epidemics of typhoid and influenza raged in the winters of 1891 and 1892, he sought through correspondence with Pasteur to develop a typhoid vaccine. He did not succeed, but he did make his second revelation that water from the Yan Yean reservoir was awash with typhoid germs.

While still at the Victoria Brewery, de Bavay began research into a new way of getting zinc by flotation, a hot question because all the mining companies at Broken Hill were missing out on additional fortunes through extracting 'less than half of the silver, two-thirds of the lead and virtually none of the zinc' contained in the ore they were hoisting out of the line of lode.[12] De Bavay drummed up financial support for his flotation research from Montague Cohen and his entrepreneur friend William Lawrence Baillieu—the famous 'W. L.'—a real risk taker who became a colossus of resources investment. It was this connection which prompted Cohen, when de Bavay returned from a scientific refresher tour of Europe, to induce him to switch laboratories from the Victoria to the Foster's brewery. De Bavay eventually succeeded in his flotation work, building the fortunes of Cohen and Baillieu.

De Bavay was, despite his other interests, a top brewer. He lifted Foster's production and also succeeded in making a draught lager which in 1895 was selling in more than forty pubs in the city and suburbs of Melbourne.[13] A noted brewing consultant, E. Tizzard-Walsh, proclaimed that Foster's was 'excellent', adding, 'That lager will be the beer of Australia in the near future is a safe prophecy.'[14] How right he was. But, oddly, the *Australian Brewers' Journal*, for years the advocate of a cool, light beer, had changed its mind, saying in an editorial in 1897, 'Lager has had its chance in Victoria and has failed to reach, or even approach, the public taste. . . . There is not the smallest chance of the concocted-in-Germany swill ever being acclimatised in Australia.'[15]

Montague Cohen — he and W. L.
Baillieu put the breweries together.

(Dunstan has speculated that the *Journal*'s Alfred Lawrence, who sold beer-making equipment, did a somersault to pacify the other breweries who were big advertisers with him.) At the turn of the century, de Bavay's Foster's was so popular that the brewery decided to try exporting it. The first shipment left Melbourne in 1901, for South Africa and the Boer War; a second went to Samoa.[16]

The new century was not promising for brewers. Numbers had been falling steadily despite a rising population. Here are the figures for Victoria:[17]

Year	Population	Breweries	People per brewery
1871	730,000	126	5,793
1892	1,140,000	68	16,764
1900	1,201,000	53	22,660

Given the examples we have seen of early-century takeovers and mergers among stock-and-station agents and jam manufacturers, it was a certainty that the number of brewers was set to decline further, too. The next step was a half-way house: a price cartel. The major metropolitan breweries, who had been in bruising competition with each other, formed the Society of Melbourne Brewers, which immediately agreed upon a jacked-up, uniform price structure: £2 3s 6d ($152) a hogshead of draught and 5s 3d ($18) a dozen for bottled beers, a lift of 12 per cent. If a brewery sold more than its normal quota, it had to kick back into a pool; if it sold less, it could apply for compensation. 'It must have been,' Dunstan has written, 'like keeping check on Russian missile sites.'[18] The publicans, long oppressed by stringent tied-house conditions imposed by the brewers, struck back. They launched their own rival brewery. They converted the old Abbotsford distillery beside the Yarra River, which they bought for £3,750 ($250,000), into a completely modern brewery. This co-operative sold beer at the same price as the society breweries, but publicans as both shareholders and customers stood to collect profits. Abbotsford prospered from day one, so much so that the society was obliged to reduce its prices and embark on a beer war.[19]

It was time for shrewd businessmen to go into action. Monty Cohen and W. L. Baillieu were already associates, moving into profit together with de Bavay's mineral flotation processes; they had paid him £6,583 ($460,000) for his five patents.[20] Cohen was, of course, on the board of Foster's, one of the smallest of the big six breweries, and Baillieu was on the board of Carlton, the largest.

W. L. Baillieu was the creator of a dynasty which has been 'synonymous with enterprise'.[21] His father, James, descended from a Belgian dealer in fine fabrics who had moved to London, was a cabin boy who jumped ship in 1853 and settled in Queenscliff, near the entrance to Port Phillip Bay. James fathered ten sons and three daughters who survived to maturity. W. L. was the second son and became 'the pivot around whom the family fortunes, and much else in Australia, turned'.[22] His education was elementary, and at fourteen he started work at the Queenscliff branch of Henry 'Money' Miller's Bank of Victoria. In his spare time he sailed, and a few years later, when he was a strapping fellow of 190 centimetres, he started crewing aboard the *Hygeia*, a yacht owned by Edward Latham, then proprietor of the Carlton Brewery, who had bought it in a sheriff's sale in 1865. Their relationship developed significantly, for W. L. married Latham's only daughter, Bertha Martha, and Latham, after becoming a widower, married W. L.'s sister Emma Elizabeth.

After twelve years in the bank and still only twenty-six, W. L. moved to Melbourne to grab his own piece of the land boom. The real-estate firm of Munro & Baillieu (Donald Munro was the son of a teetotal Scottish banker who later became a notoriously corrupt premier) was an immediate success; in its second year, with W. L. already a commanding auctioneer, it topped land sales for 1887 in Melbourne at £3 million ($210 million).[23] But, as Professor John Poynter has recorded: 'The young auctioneers inevitably became involved in land speculation themselves, in a business community deeply enmeshed in an intricate game in which Victorians borrowed money from London to lend to each other, unhindered by banking laws protecting society against its own financial recklessness.'[24] They crashed in 1892. W. L. disclosed, at a meeting with his creditors, debts of £48,936 ($3.7 million). It was agreed that he would pay the equivalent of 2.5 cents in the dollar. (Such private arrangements, quite impossible today, were common in the bust of the 1890s, eighty-seven being recorded in 1892 and fifty-two in 1893).[25]

Within weeks, W. L. was back in business as an auctioneer under the sign W. L. Baillieu & Co. at 375 Collins Street. (The firm survives as Baillieu Knight Frank.) He completely rebuilt his fortunes in what Professor John Poynter has described as an 'exceptionally expert recovery'.[26] He spread into many fields and made a separate fortune by buying up shares in the London Bank of Australia when they were cheap following the banking crashes of 1893, becoming a major shareholder and negotiating a merger with the English, Scottish and Australian Bank (ES & A), which is now part of the Australia and New Zealand Banking Group (ANZ). He organised his brothers Edward and Clive into the stockbroking firm of E. L. & C. Baillieu, for many years and still in the late 1980s presided over by John Madden Baillieu, the son of W. L.'s youngest brother Maurice. He served in the upper house of the Victorian Parliament for twenty-one years, many of them as a minister. And, of course, he invested in many mining projects, putting together a string of companies whose headquarters were accommodated in eight-storey Collins House, labelled ever since by the Left as 'a symbol for monopoly wealth and power'.[27] (Today, towering Collins Wales House has replaced the original opposite the Stock Exchange.) Within a dozen years of his bankruptcy, W. L. sat on the boards of the *Herald*, the fabulous Mount Morgan Gold Mining Company and the Dunlop Pneumatic Tyre Company of Australasia Limited, as well as the brewery.[28] And it was time for him to concentrate his attention on the latter.

Baillieu and Cohen decided that the big six breweries must merge to win the battle against the Abbotsford co-operative. But it was easier said than done. Dunstan has recorded: 'It was a long, agonised battle which took two years, a battle sorting out shareholders and debenture holders both in Australia and England, tortuous debt problems covering leases of property, mortgages on hotels and deciding which of the six flourishing breweries were to be closed down for ever.'[29] Then, in May 1907, the new combine of Carlton and United Breweries Pty Ltd (CUB) was registered with £1 million ($68 million) nominal capital in one-pound shares, the paid-up capital distributed as follows:

Brewery	Number of Shares
Carlton Brewery Ltd	80,000
McCracken's City Brewery Ltd	37,000
Victoria Brewery Pty Ltd	33,500
Castlemaine Brewery Co. (Melbourne) Ltd	20,500
Shamrock Brewing and Malting Co. Ltd	14,500
The Foster Brewing Co. Pty Ltd	14,500

Cohen and Baillieu were both on the new board, and it became something of a family affair for the next three-quarters of a century: Monty Cohen's seat passed to his son Brigadier Harold Edward Cohen (the first Jewish boy to attend Xavier College) and then to Harold's son (Sir) Edward; Baillieu's seat passed to his brother Clive (of E. L. & C. Baillieu), then to Clive's son Marshall Lawrence Baillieu (long-time chairman of North Broken Hill and other mining companies launched by W. L.) and in 1946 to W. L.'s nephew, John Madden Baillieu, who is still closely involved.[30]

On the executive side, Emil Resch—a German born in Württemberg, who learned the brewing arts in Stuttgart—was appointed general manager of the new CUB. He had made his reputation as the owner and brewer of the Lion Brewery at Silverton, twenty-five kilometres northwest of Broken Hill in far-western New South Wales, when that town boasted ten hotels and its own stock exchange and miners were getting up to ten thousand ounces of silver from each ton of ore and silver was worth four shillings ($13) an ounce. When the silver ran out (Silverton is today a ghost town—and a tourist and film-making attraction), Resch moved to Melbourne as brewer for the Victoria Brewery. His career was cut short by anti-German sentiment during World War I, even though he was a naturalised Australian. The CUB directors fired him with a golden handshake of £3,000 ($160,000), which was not ungenerous.[31] The splendid de Bavay, by then a consultant to the Swan Brewery in Western Australia and the Cascade Brewery in Tasmania—both Cohen and Baillieu interests—exchanged his long-term contract with Foster's for a consultancy with CUB. (He went on, early in World War I, to develop a way of making acetone, a key ingredient for the powerful explosive cordite, out of molasses; he also helped to found the paper-making industry in Australia. He died in 1944.)[32]

World War I saw the advent of two astonishing social decisions affecting the breweries. First, in an effort to reduce the impact of alcohol on war production, hotel licensing hours of 6 a.m. to 11.30 p.m. were cut, originally in 1915 to 9.30 p.m. and then in 1916 to 6 p.m. This had the immediate effect of boosting beer consumption and the long-term effect (forty-nine years!) of the notorious Melbourne 'six o'clock swill', in which people sought to drink as many glasses of beer as possible between knocking off work at 5 p.m. and the beer being turned off at 6 p.m. Secondly, as a genuflection to the noisy temperance lobby, barmaids were banned because they were seen as temptresses to young soldiers. They did not return until the middle of World War II when they were seen as replacements for barmen who could serve usefully in the armed forces. A nice contradiction.[33]

Carlton and United hit the takeover trail in the 1920s, buying out Hodges Brewery in Geelong in 1924 for £130,000 ($4.7 million), Fitzgerald's Brewing and Malting Company in Castlemaine in January 1925 (and closed it down), and the following month Cohn Bros Victoria Brewery in Bendigo for £120,000 ($4.3 million). But the big one came in April 1925, thanks again to the negotiating skills of Monty Cohen. His law firm of Pavey, Wilson & Cohen announced the merger of CUB and the bitter rival Abbotsford, CUB to hold two-thirds of the shares and the co-operative one-third. The directors paid Cohen—for 'the continued success of his schemes, both in politics and trade'—a special fee of £10,000 ($360,000).[34] As well they might, for virtually all competition in Melbourne and the rest of Victoria had been eliminated.

But monopoly always presents opportunities. The opportunist in 1929 was the hop merchant Peter Grant Hay (father-in-law of Sir Rupert Clarke), who built a spanking new brewery in Richmond and launched Tiger beer, triggering a sales war comparable with 1904. CUB, with a host of tightly tied hotels, were confident that they would knock off the upstart within months, but Richmond battled on for more than thirty years, always much weaker than the combine, but a nettle in its side. In the end CUB bought Richmond for an undisclosed price.[35]

The Great Depression of the early 1930s slashed beer sales by nearly a quarter, but this did not deter CUB from looking for expansion into northern Queensland, where the tropical climate stimulated the thirst

Reginald Fogarty — recognised by one and all as the Beer Baron.

for beer. It bought control of Northern Australian Breweries in Cairns, which had been struggling against under-capitalisation for its first seven years. This purchase had two direct results: it gave the company a useful supply base to cater for the needs of hundreds of thousands of thirsty soldiers, Australian and American, who trained, rested or transited in the far north after the Japanese had pushed as far south as New Guinea in World War II; and it introduced to the company Reginald Francis Graham Fogarty, a business titan for good and ill.

Fogarty came from the tropical never-never. He was born at Normanton, on the Gulf of Carpentaria just below the 17th parallel, when it served prospectors who came by sea to try their luck on the Croydon goldfield, 150 kilometres to the south-east. There was not much in the way of schooling up there, but Fogarty honed his natural organising skills in the AIF during World War I, becoming adjutant of the 11th Field Artillery. Ten years after that war, years he spent as a travelling salesman throughout Queensland, an artilleryman comrade and a director of the struggling Cairns brewery, Tony Devine, took Fogarty at his word when he said in a bar, 'I'll fix it for you.' Fogarty was the incumbent manager when CUB bought control, and he delivered for them. Profits for the first few years were so good that some £250,000 ($12 million) was spent on modernising the brewery.

Fogarty was a big, imposing fellow with a fine singing voice and a robust taste for the drink. His successes were recalled when CUB directors were looking for a new general manager after World War II, a man who could cut through post-war government restrictions, modernise the breweries and lift production (which had been pegged by regulation during the war) to meet an impatient public thirst. Fogarty got the job in 1949 and ruled (there is no other suitable word for it) for the next eighteen years, the last three as chairman. He certainly was a man of action. The Carlton brewery was completely rebuilt and re-equipped; so was the Abbotsford bottling plant. Production was lifted five-fold and a research laboratory set up. Fogarty opened a brewery in Darwin (where he used large 2.25-litre bottles which became famous as 'Darwin Stubbies') and in Fiji. He took over the Ballarat Brewing Company and, as already mentioned, bought the Richmond Brewery. He presided over the beer-can revolution in the late 1950s (more than two million sold in the first month), and he completely modernised city, suburban and country hotels. He was known to the public as the Beer Baron, and his employees were called Fogarty's Fusiliers. He continued to have his drinking bouts.[36]

Clearly his energy was magical. He was into every phase of operations, regularly visiting the brewing houses and bottling halls, inspecting every refurbished hotel. 'He was an absolute dictator,' recalled a former executive. 'He knew how many barrels of beer every hotel in Melbourne took, and if they cut their order, he wanted to know why.'

A successor in charge later was Louis J. Mangan, who had been Fogarty's personal assistant for some years. He, too, was extremely competent, but again 'an absolute dictator', just as his mentor had been. 'They reflected that old single-management style'[38] which inhibits the initiative of executives and destroys the ability in others to make decisions.

Fogarty died at his home in Toorak in 1967. He left his breweries in great shape. When he came south, group assets were £5 million ($120 million) and annual profit £550,000 ($13.2 million); when he died, assets stood at $90 million ($495 million)—the currency having changed from pounds to dollars in 1966—and profit at $7 million ($38.5 million). But the power of Carlton and United was soon to be proved beyond doubt. For two years a powerful consortium—Courage, Barclay & Simonds Ltd of Britain, British Tobacco Company (Australia) and some Victorian hotel owners—had been building an $8 million ($44 million) brewery at Broadmeadows, on Melbourne's north-western outskirts, to take on Foster's, Carlton, Melbourne *et al.* with Courage. The Courage cockerel insignia was given maximum advertising saturation, whetting the public's appetite for the battle if not the actual brew. Launching day for the new beer was Wednesday, 9 October 1968. Before dawn, brand new red-and-gold Courage trucks began deliveries to hotels; by dusk the attack was a failure. Why? The Courage beer tasted excellent—exactly the same as the CUB brew, in fact. As the *Sun News-Pictorial* reported, 'Frankly, it looks like Carlton, tastes like Carlton, turn me round, blindfold me, and I'd swear until the roof fell in that I was drinking Carlton.'[39] For all their financial courage, Courage did not have the courage to risk giving the customers something different, a real choice. So why should the drinkers change?

Scrappy Sir Maurice Nathan, chairman of Courage Breweries Ltd (and of Paterson's the furnishers and, later, president of the Victorian Football League) said his cockerel would get 10 per cent of the market in Victoria, probably more. Speculation was that 'the company captured between six and eight per cent shortly after launching . . . but the figure steadily fell to around the three-and-a-half to four per cent level'.[40] Courage reported a loss in the first year of $1.7 million ($8.8 million). Just before its tenth birthday, Courage surrendered, selling the brewery to Tooth & Co. of Sydney. It had failed to make a profit in any year. Carlton was the undisputed king.

Throughout the Courage campaign, Foster's was building a strong position abroad. It sold in more than forty markets, nowhere more powerfully than in Britain, where it had become something of a cult drink. One recalls the excitement during pre-lunch drinks in El Vino, in Fleet Street, the day the weekly *Private Eye* came out. This was a scabrous publication, but great fun because it libelled the mighty in most entertaining fashion. (For years its victims did not bother to sue because they believed the owners had no money to pay damages, but that changed.) The *Eye*'s most popular feature was a comic strip written by Barry Humphries and drawn by Nicholas Garland, 'The Adventures of Barry McKenzie', a gormless Australian adrift in London who was addicted to Foster's. Week after week the hero gave telling, if crude, plugs for Foster's:

'Have an ice old Fosters, you old bastard.'

'By cripes, all that ice cold Fosters has gone straight to the old feller. Am I bustin' for a nice long snakes!'

'Whacko the diddle oh! Do you see what I see? This lovely bastard stocks Fosters! Give us a couple of dozen tubes, mate, and don't spare the horses.'

'I'll be with you in two shakes of a lamb's arse, Blanchie. I just got to nip into the old utensil for a liquid laugh. It'd be a pity not to make room for a couple of lonely tubes of lovely ice cold Fosters, don't you reckon?'

'I got another half dozen tubes of Fosters stuffed down me Y-fronts. I'm that thirsty I could drink out of an Abbo's loincloth.'

'Cripes! If this bastard doesn't stock Fosters I'll drop him, so help me. I'm as dry as a nun's nasty!'[41]

And so on. Humphries built Foster's into the patois of Swinging London. (When the strips were published in book form, they were banned for years in Australia as too obscene. How times change!) Across the Atlantic, Foster's triumphed without the help of Bazza. It was promoted by sportsmen like tennis stars John Newcombe and Fred Stolle and later by Australians challenging for the America's Cup at Newport. From 1972, sales in the United States doubled every year. In 1976 a shipment of one million cans of Foster's was the biggest single consignment of foreign beer to enter the port of New York.[42]

Lou Mangan, Fogarty's disciple, became general manager in 1973 after a short interregnum by Brian Breheny, of a famous brewing family, who died from cancer at sixty. Mangan was the first cost accountant hired by CUB, and he had been with the company for twenty-two years, most of them dominated by Fogarty. Decisions at the top again became the style. Actually, power was shared by Mangan and Fred Coulstock, a scientist and production man who had introduced 24-hours-a-day bottling. An executive from that era recalled, 'Everyone kept their little area of knowledge; nobody ever exchanged anything. After management meetings, before I joined them, I used to take blokes to lunch to find out what was happening—and charge it to the company. It was the recognised thing, the only way one could find out what was happening. CUB was a set of secret societies.'[43]

Coda to PART ONE — Three Ripe Plums

We have looked at three groups of companies whose assets in the early 1970s totalled some $450 million ($2 billion). Each dominated its industry field, and all enjoyed an aura of power. Their paths had been curiously similar. Elder Smith Goldsbrough Mort had derived early energy and drive from Thomas Elder, Robert Barr Smith, Richard Goldsbrough and Thomas Mort but had slowed to a walk under the heavy, centralised hand of Norman Giles. Henry Jones IXL enjoyed great growth under its namesake but became geriatric under A. W. Palfreyman. Carlton and United, put together brilliantly by Montague Cohen and W. L. Baillieu, lost much of its corporate verve under the monolithic control of R. F. G. Fogarty. All three boardrooms had become more clubs than cabinets.

The three giants, for that is what they were in their fields, were perceived by the business community and the public as invincible. But they were, in truth, Goliaths. A meeting with their David was inevitable.

PART TWO

Exciting Explosions

chapter **4**
John Elliott Launches His Team

Trevor Kennedy, editor-in-chief of Australian Consolidated Press, was given time by his boss, Kerry Packer, to go off and talk to seventeen people whom he identified as world leaders in their fields—people such as Lee Kuan Yew, Harry Oppenheimer, Isaac Stern, Jack Nicklaus, and two women, Katharine Graham and Estee Lauder. In the book of those interviews,[1] he suggested what was the basic difference between the majority of intelligent, healthy and talented people and his heroes and heroines: 'Their essential ingredient to success in life is lack of fear. . . . This lack of fear is a commonsense way of talking about two things: the ability to handle ambiguity and the ability to make your own rules.' The two Australians in his fearless seventeen are Rupert Murdoch and John Elliott.

John Dorman Elliott's background was sound, secure but not spectacular—a reflection of middle Australia. He was born to Frank and Anita Elliott on 3 October 1941, the eldest of three sons.[2] It was hardly a vintage year. Adolf Hitler's German forces invaded Russia and besieged Australian diggers in the desert fortress of Tobruk in North Africa, and sixty-six days after John Elliott's birth, the Japanese, without warning, sank much of the American fleet at Pearl Harbor in Hawaii, turning World War II into a fully global affair. At home, the family's favourite football team, Carlton, finished third in the VFL competition.

Frank Elliott was then twenty-eight, the son of a Scottish-born railway engineer who worked at the Newport workshops and raised a family of six in the seaside suburb of Williamstown in Melbourne's west. Frank won a place at Melbourne High School, which then had competitive entry, and was glad to get a job with the English, Scottish and Australian Bank, for he had grown up during the hardships of the Great Depression of the 1930s and recognised that banks were secure, if

Anita and Frank Elliott — they met through their church.

unexciting, employers.[3] Frank was a teller, aged twenty-seven, when he and Anita Dorman were married at St Paul's Anglican church in Kew. They had met through the church, singing in the choir and playing tennis. Anita was born on a wheat farm in northern Victoria, the second of four daughters of Edwin John Dorman and his wife of German descent. This Edwin Dorman, originally a saddler, was a strong, barrel-chested fellow of enormous stamina who also had business nous and was a good judge of character—qualities the family say have passed to his grandson John. Edwin had decided that there had to be an easier way of making a living than trudging behind a plough in the heat of the day through a cloud of dust stirred up by a team of Clydesdales, so he bought a bakery, first at Corowa on the River Murray and then a bigger one in Melbourne. In time he became one of Victoria's biggest bakers. On the advice of his flour supplier, Harold Darling—grandson of Adelaide's John Darling and then chairman of BHP as well as John Darling & Son—he cashed up before the Depression struck, thereafter investing in likely milling and baking operations. The family lived in some style in Hawthorn. Anita went to Tintern Church of England Girls' Grammar School and then Scott's Business College and worked for the Taxpayers' Association of Victoria before her marriage.[4]

The Elliotts had just moved into their new red-brick home in Kew when John was born. He grew up there, and his parents still live in it. In his early years there was wartime food and clothing rationing, but nothing too onerous; life was tranquil as brothers Ross and Richard arrived. But a crisis developed when John was six. In his left heel he developed osteomyelitis (from the Greek *osteon*, bone; *myelos*, marrow; *-itis*, inflammation),[5] an infection that frequently led to amputation and sometimes to death. It was fortunate for him that penicillin—the magical antibiotic which, thanks to the work of Australian researcher Howard Florey, revolutionised much of medicine—was available to civilians quite soon after the end of World War II. Even so, the boy had a hard time. He had to wait in hospital for a fortnight, in acute pain, before surgeons could open the heel and scrape away the infected bone. Then for nine months he had to stay in bed or in a wheelchair while further bone fragments worked their way out. He recalled later, 'One doctor told me I wouldn't be able to walk, and I walked; he said I wouldn't be able to play football, and I played football; then he said I wouldn't be able to kick with my left foot, and I did that.'[6] The long and frustrating recovery was helped, in part, by grandfather Edwin Dorman, with whom John played cards and talked and learned, in the way the very young do with the very old.

Frank and Anita Elliott had determined early that their boys would have the best education they could afford; indeed, for some years they ran a milk bar together to cover the schooling fees, Frank doing the evening shift after his day at the bank. They chose Carey Grammar, a Baptist college a couple of kilometres from their home in Baker Avenue. John did his primary and secondary schooling at this excellent establishment, caring rather more for the team games of cricket and football than study. One master recalled later, 'His main problem in those days was lack of motivation. He always had a lot in reserve. But if you could get him interested in something, he could move mountains.'[7] Both teachers and fellow former students recall that he was a natural leader. At one time the headmaster, Stewart Hickman, was dissatisfied by the lack of verve in the singing in chapel and advised his colleagues, 'What we have to do is find the hymns that John Elliott likes best and sings lustily, and the whole school will sing with him.'[8] Such leadership qualities make school prefects, but John missed out because, in common with classmates, he was caught smoking while attending a school religious retreat in the country; that vetoed his promotion.

Saturdays were for sport, playing and watching. Frank was a Carlton fan and took his boys to as many of the Blues' games as possible during the winter. Not that being a Carlton supporter was highly rewarding during John's school years; they won the premiership in 1947 but not again for another twenty years and often missed the finals. John has recalled, 'Sport was a great influence on me. My father made sure I played competitive sports. I didn't play golf or tennis, but I played team sports—cricket and football. They were great; you learn to take defeat on the chin and to win graciously. Success is dependent on team work.'[9] Sundays were for church and family and friends. 'My father was a very religious man. I went to church. . . . I believe in it all, but I don't go very often—probably only Easter and Christmas. But I used to go every Sunday until I was about twenty-three. Maybe I went to church too often when I was young.'[10]

During his early secondary-school years, John gave a fairly low priority to work but did consider what career he might follow. For a time he toyed with becoming a radio announcer, perhaps because he did impersonations of race-callers rather well. But in time an interest in business developed, and he started to follow the stock market just as other boys become interested in racing form. He came to realise, too, that his prospects would be coloured by performance and that it would be wise to go to university. This transformed his approach to school work. In his matriculation year, the sluggish student gave it his best shot. 'I could see that my opportunities were going to be determined by how well I did.'[11] He did very well indeed: two scholarships to the University of Melbourne. One, a Commonwealth Scholarship, paid his fees (this was before the Whitlam government made tertiary education free); the other, a BHP scholarship, gave him £180 ($2,400) a year to live on.

He embarked on a course in commerce, the accountants' discipline, which normally takes three years. At the end of his second year, as one of the top fifteen students in economics, he was invited by the university to stay for a further year and tackle an honours rather than a pass degree, which he did. John Elliott's results and the recollections of his fellows placed him as an above-average student, but not brilliant; he got third-class honours. (During one examination he left the room for a quarter of an hour with one of the supervisors, explaining afterwards that he felt like a cigarette!)[12] He tended to leave assignments until the last moment, to free himself for other undergraduate activities, including football and cricket. He also reactivated the Commerce Students' Society, not least because there was a grant of £150 ($1,800) a year to be claimed plus an office in which he and his friends could study and/or play cards. He recalls, 'The big things were the footy matches against the law students. We had John Birt, who is still associated with Essendon, on the Commerce team, while Bill Serong, of Collingwood, and John Winneke played for Law.'[13] To boost his funds, Elliott and a friend launched a coaching college aimed at boys and girls who were then Leaving Certificate and Matriculation students. They put pamphlets in letterboxes round the eastern suburbs of Melbourne, and when people phoned in they advertised on the university notice boards for suitable teachers from the student body. 'We were the organisers. We made a few bob. It was my entrée into a business enterprise.'[14] As one of the four holders of a BHP scholarship, he was obliged to do vacation work for the Big Australian, clerking and visiting the works in Newcastle. His only real holiday was a fortnight with friends in a rented house at Point Lonsdale in high summer.[15]

Elliott graduates — honours in Commerce and then an MBA.

After graduating, Elliott followed through and worked for BHP, but he quite soon found the big, highly bureaucratic organisation frustrating and could see no hope of early promotion to a testing executive job. After just a couple of years he resigned and joined the management accounting firm of Watson Webb and Associates. This enabled him to embark upon his next target project: a master's degree in business administration. The idea of higher education for businessmen is a post–World War II concept; it established its first roots in the United States when American management was perceived as the best in the world. The Harvard Business School, part of the great university in Boston, was the first to establish a strong reputation for its MBAs, perhaps because its syllabus was very much marketing oriented and concentrated on case studies.[16] (Not everyone approved of the upsurge in business colleges. One critic commented, 'For years they have been turning out MBAs who, because of their training, fancy they could manage anything because they know the numbers.')[17] In Australia, Sydney led the way in the early 1960s with the Australian Graduate School of Management, which awarded MBAs; Melbourne quickly followed, and this allowed Elliott to do a part-time year of his MBA while at Watson Webb. A research grant by the University of Melbourne enabled him to switch to full-time study, and he joined the MBA class of 1965 in which more than eighty applied for places but only nineteen were chosen.[18]

As in America, MBA courses in Australia are hothouse affairs requiring concentrated study and effort, but Elliott, ever confident, still found time for other things, as his long-time friend Peter Lawrence—now managing director of stockbrokers Roach Tilley Grice & Co.—recalled: 'Some people were doing a lot of work on assignments, re-writing and really getting them perfect. But that wasn't John's style. He was more likely to be playing football, going to the races or having a few pots or whatever.'[19] Much more important, soon after the start of that academic year, he married.

Elliott met the bright and beautiful Lorraine Golder during their undergraduate days (she was voted Miss Freshette in her first year), and they had been going out together for four or five years. They were married in the Ashburton Anglican church in May 1965 and had their reception at the distinctly non-social Victoria Hotel in Little Collins Street. Elliott was twenty-three, and the newlyweds set up home in a rented house in suburban Balwyn.

An event of significance during the MBA course was a guest lecture by Roderick Carnegie, himself an MBA from Harvard and then principal of McKinsey & Co. in Australia. (McKinsey, born of the MBA revolution in American management, is the most highly regarded firm of independent management consultants in the world.) In addition to restructuring many top corporations in the United States, including Ford, it was invited to reorganise the British Post Office and Royal Dutch Shell, and in Australia its clients include the National Australia Bank, BHP and CSR. Not everyone thinks they are great; the cynical Professor C. Northcote Parkinson has written that there are only two reasons why companies call them in: 'On the one hand they may want scapegoats for the reorganisation upon which they have already decided. On the other they may want to prevent such a reorganisation taking place.'[20] A more recent perspective gave the following assessment: 'In the sixties it was McKinsey, through young Rod Carnegie, which injected American management style into Australian companies where boards previously had aped the clubby British style of muddling through.'[21] Carnegie, who obviously kept an eye out for likely talent, told Elliott's class that McKinsey found its recruits only from the top 10 per cent of

Sir Rod Carnegie (courtesy of the Melbourne Herald).

business-school graduates round the world. This meant that in a class of fewer than twenty, only two would have a chance. Elliott resolved to be one of them. Thus spurred, he lifted his game. His thesis on company comparisons lifted him to second place at the end of the course, and he went and knocked on Carnegie's door. Carnegie recalls why he took Elliott on as only the second non-US-trained consultant in the Melbourne office: 'We always took young people. He would have been twenty-four. He was Australian and he had not spent a lot of time outside the country. And he was aggressive, he was able, and he was ambitious—obviously wanted to work hard. I thought he was going to be a highly talented person.'[22]

Elliott was to spend six years with McKinsey. 'Fresh out of business school, he gained access to the senior echelons of Australian commerce while developing invaluable problem-solving skills.'[23] The first three years saw him down mines at Broken Hill and Mt Isa, investigating chemical and food processing plants, studying coal-handling at Port Kembla and through all kinds of retail shops. 'My position with McKinsey gave me not only enormous experience,' he explained, 'but showed me how big companies work and allowed me to cut through all the layers and see what was going on at the top level.'[24]

One particular assignment was to be of lasting value. It concerned Sir Ian McLennan, then shortly to become chairman of BHP. McLennan, a brilliant businessman with an engineering background, was spotted early in his career at BHP by the great Essington Lewis and became a senior executive at the age of thirty-eight. He was chief general manager at fifty and would have quickly become chairman had not some of the outside directors feared that his domination of the company was already too strong.[25] He asked McKinsey's to have a look at the family flour-milling business; the McLennans had owned and operated a flour mill at Mooroopna, in northern Victoria, since 1886, but the days of independent millers were running out. The McKinsey team, led by Elliott, put forward a scheme to combine three famous family mills—the McLennans' in the country and the Kimptons' and the Minifies' in Melbourne. For his role in the merger, Elliott was later invited to join the board of Kimpton, Minifie and McLennan Limited (KMM), which became a powerful milling and stockfeed company. More important, the young man had friends in Sir Ian McLennan and Stephen Kimpton.

The next move saw Elliott and his wife flying off to Chicago, where McKinsey's had a large office servicing the Midwest and parts of Canada. Carnegie recalls, 'I had a particularly close colleague in charge of the Chicago office, Jack Cardwell, and I was sure John and Lorraine would find the area congenial. I also wanted to make certain that we had links from Australia in McKinsey offices other than New York and San Francisco.'[26] Elliott became part of a team advising retailers, particularly the Gamble-Skogmo supermarket chain run by Jim Watson.

Sir Ian McLennan — always a strong man in takeover negotiations.

Management consultancy is primarily concerned at boardroom level with the reorganisation of company structures and chains of command,[27] but the essential preliminary research on the ground turns a consultant 'into a company detective, looking for clues.'[28] Elliott's research into Watson's supermarkets and discount stores, then the eighth largest retail group in the United States, took him into a store somewhere in Arizona where he saw a whole department stocked with fishing tackle although there was not a lake or likely water within a day's drive. The problem was that head office dictated the product line for each store instead of allowing local managers to stock only things they could sell. By changing such practices, and by selling off $20 million worth of idle stock, the Elliott team lifted Watson's profits by 50 per cent in the first year, and the share price took off from $18 to $44![29]

During some eighteen months in Chicago, Elliott reached two con-clusions. First, a long-term career as a consultant was not what he wanted; he had the drive to run his own business. Secondly, he did not want his children, who had started to arrive, to grow up in America; he wanted them to have the benefits of the Australian environment. When discussing his conclusions with Jim Watson, the American tycoon offered to bankroll him to a million dollars in an Australian enterprise.[30]

Elliott spent 1971 back with McKinsey & Co. in Melbourne—and joined the Liberal Party.[31] He has recalled that Ron Fowler, of Fowlers Vacola, took him to the annual meeting of the Canterbury branch of the party at which delegates, one man and one woman, to state council were elected. 'Out of the blue, Ron said he would like to nominate me for the job. . . . Suddenly I came from nowhere to being a state dele-gate.'[32] The Liberals certainly needed new blood. They had ruled Aus-tralia continuously for twenty-two years, the first seventeen of them under the successful leadership of Robert Gordon Menzies, the later years under the de-escalating quality of Harold Holt, John Gorton and finally William McMahon, who was to be annihilated a year later by Gough Whitlam and Labor.[33] Fresh thinking on issues and policies was urgently required, and Elliott was prepared to become 'heavily involved'. (His earliest political skirmishes had been at university, when, of his group of fifteen who went the honours route, only he and one other supported the Liberal Party. 'The other thirteen were avid Labor people. The universities were anti-government.'[34])

Elliott's major preoccupation during 1971 was setting up to have a go on his own. He mapped out a clear strategy. He would assemble backers for, and then identify, a company that could be acquired for $10 million ($45 million). 'I sought people who would be in for the long haul. No good finding a company and then having to raise the money to buy it.'[35] But his first call on the backers would be for $50,000 to finance him through the search. The $50,000 would pay for a secretary and provide him with a carry-on salary for a year, at much less than he was earning at McKinsey. His friend Peter Lawrence, by then a partner in stockbrokers Roach & Co. (now Roach Tilley Grice & Co.), arranged for him to use an office in the partners' Collins Street premises. Work began there in February 1972, when Elliott was thirty.

His first financial recruit was Carnegie, who had returned from McKinsey's in New York as heir-apparent at the mining company Conzinc Riotinto of Australia in Melbourne. With his friend Sidney Baillieu ('Bails') Myer, whom Elliott did not then know, Carnegie had 'a small venture capital company' (Enterprise Management),[36] which was run by Dr Timothy Pascoe, an academic from Adelaide who got his PhD at Cambridge and his MBA at Harvard and was with McKinsey for four years. At Carnegie's urging, Enterprise Management promised support.

Elliott then approached the Kimpton brothers, Stephen and Roger, of KMM. Stephen MacDonald Kimpton (Melbourne Grammar and Brasenose College, Oxford, and a gallant officer during World War II) was a professional company director, the deputy chairman of the Commercial Bank of Australia (CBA—now part of the Westpac Banking Corporation) and a director of the National Mutual Life Association of Australasia. His role proved crucial. For not only was Kimpton family money committed, but he introduced Ellliott to the CBA and later to National Mutual. The first meeting with CBA executives was not fruitful, so Kimpton arranged for Elliott to meet the bank's directors, including James Balderstone, at their Christmas luncheon in December 1971. 'I made my pitch to the full board right after lunch, and they showed strong interest. I put it to them that I was looking for four blocks of twenty-five per cent of ten million dollars with which to buy a company. They agreed to be in it. Then Stephen Kimpton said, 'Now I'll take you to National Mutual.'[37] National Mutual, through Huntly Walker, who was an actuary and chief executive, put the second 25-per-cent block in place. Then Tim Pascoe said, 'I know Skinny Giles [then chairman of Elders GM] well—he and my father fought together in World War One.'[38] He arranged for Elliott to make a presentation to Sir Norman Giles, and he also committed. So the backing for $10 million was in place: CBA 25 per cent, National Mutual 25 per cent, Elders GM 15 per cent, and the balance from Carnegie, Myer, the Kimptons and the Darling family through Gordon Darling; and Elliott had the initial $50,000 to finance his hunt. 'He began to scour the corporate landscape for companies with four attributes he considered to be the *sine qua non* of prospective takeover candidates: 1. Poor management; 2. High asset level; 3. Turnaround potential; 4. A price tag of less than $10 million [$44 million].'[39] During a five-month campaign of twelve-to-fourteen-hour days in his little Roach office, he analysed more than three hundred Australian companies, realising along the way that nothing was left in the $10 million range and he would have to go higher.

By the start of the winter of 1972, Elliott's prime target was the jam and fruit canner Henry Jones IXL. The company, as we have seen, was on a downward slide under the dead hand of elderly management; earnings per share had slipped from 28.8 cents in 1963 to 19.2 cents in 1968 to 11.2 cents in 1971.[40] He code-named his prospect Tiger and 'did enough work to know Henry Jones better than anyone in the company itself'.[41] Obviously Henry Jones IXL had been spotted by others beforehand. The British takeover specialists Slater Walker had started to build a stake in it, and this had stirred the biggest shareholder, Perpetual Trustees Australia Ltd, with 7 per cent, to press for some rejuvenating action. At a stormy shareholders' meeting in June 1972, the Trustees insisted that McKinsey & Co. and Darling and Co. (the merchant bank founded by John Darling, great-grandson of Adelaide's

Stephen Kimpton — made the vital introductions.

'Grain King', and brought to prominence by James D. Wolfensohn, now a leading New York financier) be brought in both to smarten up and to defend the company. At the same time, Eastralian, another raider, started buying Henry Jones shares, forcing the price up from $2.70 to $3.40. The *Age* reported, 'Mystery Holding Grows'. Some three hundred thousand shares accumulated over three months through ANZ Nominees.[42]

Elliott decided on two courses of action: he bought on market 232,700 Henry Jones shares at an average price of $3.26 ($3.31 after brokerage) for a total of $770,000 ($3 million), $7,500 of it his own money and the rest borrowed; and 'after long deliberation' he met with Tiger. At the first meeting, with Alan M. Robinson, the chairman, and David B. Palfreyman, his deputy and son of old A. W., he was invited to visit South Africa to look over the company's operation there.[43] He went at once, taking with him a copy of a letter from Robinson to the chairman in South Africa which said *in toto*: 'Please give this man every consideration and help.' It proved magical. The South African director told him, 'I don't know who you are, son, but the chairman hasn't written to me for twelve years, so you must be important.'[44] What he saw was encouraging; the plants in South Africa were much more modern than those in Australia, explaining in part why operations there, with one-third of the company's total assets, were generating more than half of group profits.[45] He also discovered that Harry Oppenheimer's diversified mining giant, Anglo American Corporation, was interested in the business and had, after a detailed review, made an offer at a large discount for Tiger's whole South African enterprise; it had been rejected out of hand.

Elliott met again with Palfreyman, who had become chairman upon the death of Robinson while Elliott was in South Africa, and also with the full board of Henry Jones. The talks were friendly, but he was well aware that he was dealing with a largely do-nothing board. Action was called for. But first he had to escalate his backers' commitment from $10 million to a more realistic $30 million. The key man was Douglas William Stride, at sixty-one the recently appointed managing director of CBA, a Ballarat boy who had spent his life with the bank. Elliott had to win a man who was twice his own age, a bowls enthusiast and cautious! The challenge was compounded by the fact that AJC, a big part of Henry Jones, banked with the CBA, and bankers are notoriously diffident about tampering with a client's business. Elliott fronted in Stride's office and told him that the taking of Henry Jones 'looked like the best deal I'd ever seen.' Stride responded, 'They are hopeless. I'll support you.'[46]

By this time Elliott had established the corporate entity General Management Holdings. 'We called it GMH for the heck of it,' he said. 'After BHP, General Motors Holden was the biggest company in Australia, so we called our company GMH'[47] He had also secured the services of Richard Wiesener, a man of much his own age with whom he had shared his first office at McKinsey and an 'intellectual financial engineer'.[47] (Wiesener's father was killed before he was born; he was one of the pilots of the RAAF Hudson which crashed on approach to Canberra in August 1940, killing Army Minister G. A. Street, Air Minister J. V. Fairbairn and several senior officers.)

Knowing that he had Stride on side, Elliott prepared a thirty-seven-page strategy document for all his backers. 'Taking Tiger by the Tail', written at the end of July 1972, was actually an agenda paper for a meeting with them. 'I had to sell the whole thing in reverse,' Elliott explained, 'demonstrating it was a "no lose" situation—that, no matter how badly I ran it, they were still going to make money.'[48] It spelled out a four-year program which would generate—from asset sales, net depreciation and after-tax profits—some $34 million. It was convincing, and his backers agreed to make a move on Tiger at a top price of $4.50 a share, more than a dollar above current market price. The bidding vehicle was called Food Canning Industries. The first offer of $3.95 a share for half of each shareholder's investment in Henry Jones IXL was made on Friday, 24 September 1972, a partial bid of $15 million ($60 million).[49] The day saw hectic trading in Jones shares; speculators, banking on a higher follow-up offer, lifted the price by fifteen cents a share. Elliott, unperturbed, was one of 112,393 spectators at the Melbourne Cricket Ground the following day to see his beloved Carlton kick a grand-final record of 28 goals 9 behinds (177 points) to beat Richmond in an upset victory.[50] 'I stood in the outer and saw the win as being a good omen for the bid,' he said.[51]

The directors of Henry Jones did an absolutely unprecedented thing for them: they met on the Sunday. Clearly they were at sixes and sevens, because it took the old boys nine hours to put together a statement rejecting the offer; they said the shares were worth $5.50.[52] Elliott's backers showed that they were committed when the offer was raised a month later to a full bid at $4.25 a share. The Henry Jones directors meekly sought $4.30, but the deed was done; shareholders rushed to collect their cash after so many years of paltry returns, and Elliott soon had 78.7 per cent of the shares for an outlay of $33 million ($132 million).[53] Carnegie commented, 'Elliott led the field in going out on his own to identify an under-valued business; it was an adventurous move at that time, although others did it later.'

Elliott and the elegant Wiesener moved into their new corporate headquarters at 20 Garden Street, South Yarra, just across the road from the giant bluestone cannery, at the start of 1973. 'They were totally different,' recalled Barbara A'Beckett, their secretary. 'Elliott was always the leader, Wiesener always the follower. Every day for five years they arrived at the office together. Elliott would walk in first with

Richard ambling on behind. Richard was sophisticated, an urbane sort of gentleman, a soft man.'[54] They were joined at once by a brilliant young man of twenty-seven who already had a top track record in the food business. Peter Damian Scanlon had joined the H. J. Heinz company immediately after taking first-class honours in commerce at the University of Melbourne and within six years had become the local general manager. Why did he switch? 'I wanted to work for an Australian-based public company as distinct from a branch office of a foreign corporation; they asked me and it seemed reasonable.'[55] The founding team was filled out that January by the hiring on a three-months-trial basis of Barbara A'Beckett; fifteen years later she recalled, 'I had lived in Rome, London and Zambia and then separated from my husband and returned here with a school-age son. I really had no idea what secretaries did.' She learned quickly, and within months had a fourth executive to look after: Bob Cowper, the former Test cricketer and a friend of Elliott's since university days, who was market savvy through years with stockbrokers Guest and Bell. 'He was completely different again,' said Barbara A'Beckett; 'so quiet. Every day for ten years he would arrive at ten minutes to nine and go into his office, and you'd never know he was there.'[56]

Scanlon recalled those early days: 'John was the boss, the original entrepreneur. Richard was the financial engineer. Bob was the practical doer in the commercial market. And I was brought in as the man who knew how to run things. . . . There was certainly a sense of excitement and hard work. Barbara, who is a character in her own right, rarely used the telephone; it was all just shouting out.' And Wiesener has recalled: 'It was very exhilarating, a crazy time. We were used to working hard as consultants, but usually on one assignment, one problem at a time. At Henry Jones we were putting in long, long, long hours. The phone rang all the time. There were a thousand meetings a day. . . . It was mayhem, a terrific change from consulting, but very enjoyable.'[57]

The 'juniors', now senior executives, came from the MBA well. Elliott has said, 'We find MBAs useful because we do lots of one-time analyses. We want decisions quickly, sometimes yesterday.'[58] So he did a Carnegie and looked over the MBA class at the University of Melbourne and selected the top three: Geoffrey Frederick Lord, Kenneth C. Jarrett and Dick Marsland, a Western Australian who decided to go back to Perth after a few months of the mayhem. Lord and Jarrett, a finance specialist who worked first for Wiesener, stayed and prospered. Their initial training had been excellent. Lord had joined Ford Australia, then led by the charismatic Bill Bourke, after getting his honours degree in economics at Monash University. 'Ford was a good, tough outfit,' he recalled. 'Disciplinarians. The day I joined them I worked until midnight. It made an impression.'[59] Within five years he had reached second-management, and Ford paid for his MBA course. 'At the end of the

MBA year I had three options: go back to Ford, join McKinsey's, or go with Elliott. Unfortunately at Ford you are just a cog, so I joined Elliott.'[60] Lord was then twenty-seven.

Jarrett, a bachelor of commerce and a fellow of the Australian Society of Accountants, had spent two years with Alcoa—'an excellent company; they teach you properly. I had eight jobs in my two years.'[61] During his MBA course he found that 'the whole class really wanted to work for Elliott. . . . The MBA program is all about reviving rundown companies, and that is what he was into.' Jarrett joined at twenty-nine, and he remains nostalgic about the early days: 'It used to be a very tight-knit team—drinks in the boardroom on Friday night, and you'd actually discuss problems and come to some sort of consensus. You benefited a lot from talking with other people.'[62]

Another 'junior' to join within the year was Peter Tasman Bartels, who is actually nine months older than Elliott. He was the only non-academic; his schooling finished at Box Hill High School. His passion was bicycle racing, and he won the gold medal for the 1,000-metres time trial at the Commonwealth Games in Perth in 1962 when he was twenty-one. 'But he realised that there were far more opportunities in business than bikes,' a colleague recalled.[63] 'So he joined Abbott Laboratories, the American drug company, as a salesman and then moved to a higher position at Drug Houses of Australia (DHA). He was general manager there by the time he was thirty.' Bartels was not sought, but walked in and asked Elliott for a job. 'He had good practical training, and we welcomed him,' Elliott said.[64] That was the group that set about breathing new life into the moribund Henry Jones IXL.

Elliott had written in his first strategy paper on Tiger that 'the overriding opportunity to free up assets and improve profits comes from plant rationalisation—reducing plants from seventeen down to two, thus freeing up valuable properties and eliminating outdated plant and methods with efficient canning and jam-making facilities.'[65] This was put in hand immediately, with some surprises: Wiesener telephoned Elliott from Tasmania to report that they owned an apple-processing plant at Huonville which they had never heard of. When Elliott questioned the head Henry Jones man in Hobart the next day, he was told, 'Oh yes, I forgot to tell you about that.'[66] When word spread that they were selling unwanted properties, people went to the Hobart office trying to buy places the new owners knew nothing about. Elliott recalled: 'Over the years, when a fruit grower went broke, Henry Jones took over the property and wrote off the rest of the debt. The properties just sat there, because they never sold anything.'[67] Efforts to find properties not listed in the company records were made more difficult because in the Tasmanian Titles Office they were entered in the name of the property first followed by the name of the owner, not in the name of the owner first. There were other strange things. Workers who were detailed to clear out a warehouse in South Yarra found the place to be totally flea infested.[68] And, of course, a new management structure had to be put in place. Scanlon recalled his first visit to the Hobart operation: 'There were still people standing up at slanted desks with quill pens. All their systems and books were still kept by hand. I had no comprehension that it still existed. It wasn't history—it was still there.'

Within three months of the takeover, the wider world was starting to take notice. The *Australian* reported that Henry Jones was 'undergoing skilful surgery in the hands of its new owners'.[69] Christopher Skase, clearly more capable as an entrepreneur than a writer, told his readers in the *Australian Financial Review*, 'Long the fruit and jam canner, Henry Jones IXL Ltd is planning its first break with traditional activities under new management with a multi-million-dollar retail complex on the site of an existing cannery.'[70] And in a first major profile in a series in the *Australian* called 'The Go Getters', John Hurst showed how easy it was to misjudge matters: 'John Elliott is a good illustration of how to succeed in business without really trying.[71] Elliott was trying like hell.

The new team went formally on parade on 28 March 1973 at the company's sixty-third annual general meeting and the extraordinary general meeting that followed. The accounts under review were all pre-takeover, being to the year ending 30 September 1972. The meeting enabled the shareholders to approve the six new directors: executives Elliott, Wiesener and Scanlon and non-executives Timothy Marcus Clark (representing the CBA as biggest shareholder and also the chairman), Huntly Gordon Walker (of National Mutual Life) and Bails Myer.[72] The extraordinary meeting saw the capital reorganised, so that ninety-nine cents of each one-dollar share 'being in excess of the needs of the company' were returned to investors and a bonus issue converted each one-dollar share into three fifty-cent shares.[73] And the annual report, circulated to the three thousand shareholders who owned the balance of Henry Jones after Food Canning Industries, gave Elliott a platform to tell them of his plans: 'Our objective is to utilise the skills and resources of Henry Jones in an optimum manner so that the group: achieves rapidly growing returns for stockholders; develops as a force in the Australian business community; provides increasing opportunities for staff members.'[74] It must be said, more than fifteen years later, that Elliott has stuck to those clear objectives, realised them beyond reasonable expectation, and continues to push them.

The founding four were young and optimistic; they felt sure they could fix Henry Jones. But, being intelligent, they did some serious thinking about the ongoing business and decided that they must either build it or get out of it. The question was: Can we get out of it; will somebody buy it? Elliott decided to go and see the legendary Tony O'Reilly and find out. Anthony J. F. O'Reilly—Dublin born, a law graduate from Ireland's University College and an international Rugby Union

The old Jam Factory circa 1916.

player—had joined Heinz-Erin at thirty-one and by 1972, aged thirty-six, was executive vice-president and chief operations officer at the H. J. Heinz Company's world headquarters at Pittsburgh, Pennsylvania. Elliott made an appointment to visit him, but it did not work out quite as planned. As he recalled, 'Soon after I arrived, his lovely Irish secretary said, "Tony's on the phone for you." I took it, and he said, "I'm sorry, but we've had to put the plane down on the way from New York, and I won't be with you until after lunch. So just you take over the place and start running it." I said, "Fine", and called in all his staff and said to them, "Tell me what is going on in this place." They were understandably baffled, so we had a chatty lunch together.'[75] He added: 'Heinz should have bought Henry Jones. It enhanced their Australian business. But in the end they didn't.' So the four decided that they would have to find a modern factory if they were to survive.

Elliott's biographer has written that the sell-off of Henry Jones's unwanted assets in 1973 'was a fire sale the like of which had not been seen since the great receiverships of the Depression years'.[76] Some $5 million ($20 million) was realised in the first eight months by the sale of more than a hundred properties in Australia. Then came two very significant deals, one a sale, the other a purchase.

Operations in South Africa were making most of the company's money, but there was too much invested there. Elliott decided that, in order to make his whole exercise pay, he would have to sell South Africa at a good price. He and Wiesener set out on the first of eight selling flights. They ferreted out a considerable character, Jan Picard, a famous former Springbok Rugby player who was running Brink Broers Beleggings Beperk (the Brink Group). He was prepared to buy the fruit and jam canning operations, with such popular brands as IXL, Silver Leaf and All Gold, but not the pineapple operations, which were losing money. The deal was done for $12 million ($48 million). But it was almost impossible to move large amounts of money out of South Africa. However, perhaps because Picard was married to the daughter of the Finance Minister and perhaps because the buyers were Afrikaner rather than the more usual English businessmen, they were able to repatriate $10 million—the biggest sum got out to that time and maybe even since—and put the balance into preferred stock in Picard's company.[77] (The night the deal was signed, Elliott selected the most expensive, and best, claret on the list of the splendid Mount Nelson Hotel: Château Margaux. It cost $26.40 ($105) a bottle, and he and Wiesener drank two. 'My hobby of collecting Bordeaux wines really started that night,' he recalled.[78] He also collects antique oak furniture and silver.) Peter Bartels was sent over to run the pineapple operations and experienced a happy turn-round. The bottom fell out of Picard's fruit and jam canning, and the pineapples came good!

The purchase was close to home, an up-to-date cannery to replace the clapped-out capacity which had been sold off. The Melbourne *Herald* reported: 'Forty years ago Archibald Wilberforce Spooner started a small business mixing plum puddings in the garage of his home in Gardenvale. He started with £100 [$5,000]. The company, Tom Piper, which produces baked beans, spaghetti, sausages and vegies in cans, is valued today at $5.9 million [$20 million].'[79] Elliott bid $2.03 a share for Tom Piper's 2.8 million shares. Southern Packers, a near-neighbour of Tom Piper in Port Melbourne, counter-bid at $2.20. Elliott delivered the *coup de grace* at $2.35, and the famous brand and the plant and equipment were his for $6.8 million ($23 million).[80]

The books were ruled off on 30 September 1973 to mark the effective end of the Elliott team's first year in charge. The change was impressive. The previous year's result of $1.1 million ($4.4 million) net operating profit was boosted to $2.6 million ($10.4 million), a lift of 136 per cent, and dividends paid to shareholders went up by 71 per cent to 8.1 cents a share.[81]

Despite the boisterous business activity, there was still time for play-ing football and, indeed, for politics. The long Liberal run in power in Canberra had collapsed on Saturday, 2 December 1972, when Gough Whitlam led Labor out of the wilderness. Going into 1973 the Liberal Party, as Carnegie recalls, 'was in a major state of shock, and a few of us felt they needed a better research effort.'[82] It became something of a McKinsey old boys' project; in addition to Elliott and Carnegie, there were Jim Carlton—then the secretary of the New South Wales division of the party and now the MHR for MacKellar, who had been a McKinsey consultant 1966–71—Timothy Pascoe and, indeed, Richard Wiesener. Carlton began work on the restructuring of the federal secretariat with two of the brighter 'dries' from Western Australia: John Hyde, who was to become MHR for Moore for a while, and Peter Shack, an honours graduate from the University of Western Australia who was to win, and still holds, the seat of Tangney. In the end, Pascoe became federal director of the party for a couple of years and then became an adviser to Malcolm Fraser when he became prime minister. Further, Carlton called upon his former McKinsey mates to help in designing policies, fund raising and seeking good people. (Elliott told Trevor Kennedy later: 'I'm issue-related. I want to see better policies and the Party get into government and run the country better. I think Australia has been very badly run now for twenty-five years'[83]—roughly since the retire-ment of Menzies.) The need for clear policies became urgent in the autumn of 1974 when the late Sir Billy Snedden and Doug Anthony engineered a surprise federal election. Elliott had a congenial time writ-ing the primary industry policy with Tony Street, but Wiesener—actively in politics for the first and last time—had a terrible time on education policy with his shadow minister. 'Malcolm Fraser gave him hell,' said Elliott.[84] (The Whitlam Labor government was returned with a slightly decreased majority.)

The second Elliott-team year at Henry Jones was also successful, lifting net operating profit by a further 22 per cent. Chairman T. Marcus Clark reminded shareholders that—following the capital return, bonus issue and increased dividends of the first year—they had in the year to September 1974 received a one-for-five bonus issue and a dividend hike of 12 per cent.[85] And a few days after the annual meeting in March 1975, the National Times eulogised, perhaps jealously: 'Fortunes can still be made in Australia with brains and effort. And they can be made fast. Three main architects of the Henry Jones jam caper (Elliott, Wiesener and Scanlon) have been able to parlay a personal cash outlay of only $7,000 [$21,000] into personal paper worth at least $1 million [$3 million] and perhaps $1.5 million [$4.5 million] in less than three years. It has been largely tax free. . . . The Henry Jones takeover profits have also helped enrich the wealth of Rod Carnegie, the CRA chief, and Sidney 'Bails' Myer.'[86]

Little did the *National Times*, or any other outsider, know that, like Browning's thrush, the team could not recapture the first fine careless rapture of the opening years in the following two, and that net operating profits would be sticky until the late 1970s. The difficulty was a fundamental one: most of the Henry Jones business was based on fruit, and fruit growing is a notoriously unstable enterprise, buffeted by bad seasons and at the whim of consumers' tastes. It is, perhaps, the most surprising thing about Elliott's original analyses of hundreds of target companies that he picked one dependent on fruit, a decision he has since condemned: 'Our basic business was in a rotten industry, the canned fruit industry—what you learn from that is that you don't really want to get into industries that are in trouble.'[87] He has been echoed by Peter Scanlon: 'The canned fruit industry is impossible.'[88] Their vulnerability was compounded by a major change overseas. Britain had joined the European Economic Community and started changing its buying habits, a fact recorded by the prime minister of the day, Gough Whitlam: 'Britain did not purchase as many dried fruits from the Murray irrigation areas when it could easily obtain them from Greece and Turkey. It was very difficult to sell Australian canned apricots, peaches and pears to Britain when it could obtain better ones from Italy.'[89]

The problem was further compounded by the fact that a major part of Tom Piper's business, selling canned meat to Britain, vanished within months of their taking over the splendid plant. The EEC killed it. Elliott recalled 'The benefits we gained by taking all our production into that Tom Piper plant were negated by the fact that one big chunk of its traditional business—camp pie, sausages and veg, steak-and-kidney pie—simply disappeared. We were right back where we started.'[90]

It is said that pressure rarely gets to Elliott. 'I can think of only three times in fifteen years when we've had some bad times, when he's been under pressure,' Barbara A'Beckett has said. Certainly 1975 was one of them. Geoff Lord, who was then managing the hop operations and properties in Tasmania, recalled, 'He has told me that a couple of times he was close to breaking loose and taking myself and the businesses I ran as a small buy-out and going off.'[92] Elliott's personal dilemma was heightened by developments in his political life. At mid-1975 he was elected vice-chairman of the Liberal Party in Victoria and soon afterwards was offered the blue-ribbon seat of Higgins, to be vacated by former prime minister John Gorton at the next election, whenever it may be. He was much tempted. But his backers, notably the CBA, the equal-biggest shareholder, would not hear of it. The popular belief is that the bank said, 'You got us into this; now get us out.'[93] His position was made the more piquant on 11 November 1975, when the Whitlam Government was dismissed following the opposition's refusal in the Senate to pass the supply bill under which governments get the money to run the bureaucracy.

The *Sun News-Pictorial* headlined the company's 1975 results: 'Good Years Over for Henry Jones',[94] and Chanticleer commented in the *Australian Financial Review*: 'The Henry Jones (IXL) Ltd takeover dream of rationalising the Australian food industry has turned into a nightmare with the group incurring losses of more than $2 million [$5.2 million] in its food operations.'[95] To add to the team's frustrations, the bureaucrats simply would not let them press ahead with the $10 million plan to transform old Palfreyman's jam factory in South Yarra into what Christopher Skase had described in the *Financial Review* as 'a unique multi-level shopping complex'. Elliott had observed the stunning way old structures in Britain and America had been converted, and he called in architect Peter McIntyre, then the president of the Royal Australian Institute of Architects, to work out a scheme for the two-hectare site, updating the splendid bluestone structure and adding a multi-storey car park at the rear. The plans had been completed, but over and over again the authorities had stalled on the necessary rezoning. Adversity does not daunt Elliott, however; instead, it lifts his leadership qualities. Scanlon has recalled these difficult months: 'The guy was very expressive and always shared things fully. . . . It enabled us to bind together and solve the problems, rather than people being hit over the head and blamed. There were no recriminations, unless someone hid something from him—he didn't like that.'[96]

Scanlon himself was at the cutting edge, running the Food Division from Port Melbourne. The central problem was the historic conflict between the growers and the processors; the growers' co-operatives did not always have to make a profit to survive, but the processors did. Scanlon has said: 'The structure was basically with the co-operatives, which, if profitable, returned a higher price to the fruitgrowers, which meant our costs went up so that there was never any margin in it.'[97] Elliott and Scanlon worked on a strategy of rationalisation which called for the merger of the bigger co-ops and the moving of the factory from Port Melbourne to the Goulburn Valley, but the co-ops, racked by rural politics, jibbed. A solution had to wait a year or two. Across Bass Strait, things went better. Frozen food operations were merged with Cottee's General Food Ltd to create General Jones and free up plant and properties for selling off, and apple processing was sold to Clements Marshall Consolidated. The results to September 1976 showed a net operating profit of $470,000 ($1 million) although the food division lost $1.86 million ($3.6 million).[98]

All the backers were still not happy, but the corner had been turned. Since then the performance of Elliott and his team has improved year by year, spectacularly. Perhaps as an omen, the year closed with the successful rezoning of the jam factory project.[99]

Scanlon's 'strategic solution' to the Goulburn Valley fruit operations was stepped up, first with a surprise $1.54 million ($3.5 million) takeover bid for SPC, the famous canning co-op at Shepparton.[100] Strong reactions made headlines: 'IXL bid shocks growers'[101] and 'Battle erupts for the Goulburn Valley'.[102] There was clearly grower distrust of Elliott. Then came a quick switch: the SPC bid was abandoned and the company struck thirty-five kilometres west of Shepparton by buying half of the Kyabram Preserving Company for $4 million ($9 million). The switch called for secrecy. Jim Stock, who ran Kyabram, said, 'If you boys come up with a chequebook, we'll do it first thing Monday morning.'[103] Elliott recalled: 'Word went round the valley on Friday night that Henry Jones would buy the growers' shares—it was a public company but enjoyed the co-ops' tax status. Scanlon and Cowper spent the Sunday night in Shepparton and set out early on Monday morning, having heard from Stock that growers were queueing at the gate. They thought the shares were worthless. But Cowper's Jaguar broke down on the way. So they had to hail an old fellow who was bowling along in his truck with his dog on the back. Seeing them all dressed up in suits, he asked what they were doing. "We're buying the cannery," they said. "Gee, in that case I'd better give you a ride." So they rode into Kyabram cannery on the back of this old truck, clutching their chequebooks.'[104]

On more personal matters, Elliott at last stopped playing football for the Carey Old Boys at the age of thirty-five, and Richard Wiesener, who from day one had commuted from Sydney to spend Monday to Thursday at the Garden Street office, cut back to three days a week away from home.[105] Financial 1977 closed on 30 September with profits of $2.4 million ($5.4 million), a leap of 400 per cent, which 'flowed from substantial rationalisation begun late last year'.[106]

Things were well on the move. Profits for 1978 lifted again by 40 per cent to $3.3 million ($7.25 million) and in the winter of 1979 the team made what the *Age* called their 'first major takeover for six years'.[107] They made an opening bid of $20.5 million ($41 million) for Provincial Traders Holding Limited, a Queensland-based margarine and oils business which also owned a stockfeed outfit on the Darling Downs and an air-conditioning contracting business—and which had, for the betterment or otherwise of the Australian diet, launched upon the nation the ubiquitous Chiko Roll through its Victorian-registered Frozen Food Industries. The millionaire peanut grower and premier of Queensland, Johannes Bjelke-Petersen, leapt to the defence of the English owners of Provincial Traders by threatening to pass legislation to keep out the 'southern takeover merchants'.[108] His government further made noises about removing its deposits from the CBA, which made the bankers unhappy. As Elliott points out, such takeovers were still quite controversial ten years ago and not fully approved of. But the directors of Provincial Traders had no such qualms and sought no protectors. Within a month they settled for the enhanced offer of $28 million ($56 million).[109] As with many of the team's takeovers, the acquisition also yielded a crop of executives who could grow with the group, in this case notably Michael R. Nugent, then a trained accountant of thirty-five, who today is in Elliott's top team of seven executives. That financial year closed with operating profits of $4.34 million ($8.7 million), a lift of 31 per cent and a record, and the dividend to shareholders was raised from 8 cents to 10 cents a share.[110]

The year closed on a very happy note. After six years of frustration, the transformed Jam Factory was given a gala—some called it a 'galah'[111]—opening by Dame Edna Everage (Melbourne Grammar's most famous son, Barry Humphries). The luxury retailer Georges was the head tenant with splendid display windows facing Chapel Street, and a mass of boutiques and food places filled in behind; there was also parking for eight hundred cars. The complex quickly became the in place for yuppies.

The pace quickened even more in 1980. For a start, Provincial Traders' operations came into the accounts, contributing nearly $3 million ($5.4 million) to consolidated net income. Then the frozen food firm of Wattie Pict was targeted. Scanlon had shed the nightmares of the fruit co-operatives and was concentrating on business strategy with Bob Cowper, keeping tabs on twenty to thirty prospect companies. (Elliott has been strong on corporate strategy since his McKinsey days—'You've got to spend time on the strategy; I focus on the strat-

The Jam Factory — refurbished into a top shopping centre in South Yarra.

egy.'[112]) For $4 million ($7.2 million) they picked the eyes out of Wattie Pict, securing trademarks, stock and assets which almost doubled frozen foods operations and allowed profitable rationalisation.

Then a chance conversation at mid-year set in train a merger of personal as well as business significance. It will be remembered that Elliott, during his time at McKinsey, worked on the flour-milling amalgamation which produced KMM Limited. In 1978 KMM had merged with the maltsters Barrett Burston (Australia) Limited, another long-established business—the Burston family migrated from England in 1853 and bought a malt-house and in 1912 merged with the Barrett brothers. It will further be remembered that, as a result of his KMM work, Elliott went on the board as soon as he left McKinsey; he and Sir Ian McLennan were the only non-executive directors. McLennan recalls a conversation with Elliott in 1980: 'I said to John: How about Henry Jones and Burston merging?—then we would have a good sizeable company. John embraced the idea.'[113]

Friendly negotiations were started, and they made good sense; Henry Jones and Barrett Burston fitted together naturally. They were both big in stockfeed (Henry Jones through Provincial Traders); Barrett Burston's $15-million-a-year sales of cereals, flour and pet food expanded Henry Jones's range of foods and lowered the importance of fruit canning and jam making in its repertoire (although at that time the company completed its purchase of Kyabram Preserving); and, vitally, they were both suppliers to brewers at home and overseas, Barrett Burston of malt and Henry Jones of hops. (Geoff Lord had done a top job with hops in Tasmania, where he had found a number of small farmers all marketing against each other; so he had created Australian Hop Marketers Pty Ltd—'It had an official ring to it overseas'[114]—to sell their combined crop, and he had bought up all the processing units so that growers were obliged to go to him. 'We positioned ourselves,' he said, 'but it also gave them the best return.'[115] At the time of the talks with Barrett Burston, the company was expanding its hop gardens and bringing in a new one near Ulverstone at a cost of $5 million. It was also in a joint hop-growing venture with Carlton and United Breweries in north-eastern Victoria of which Elliott and CUB's Lou Mangan took turns as chairman.) In fact, Barrett Burston were the biggest maltsters in Australia and Henry Jones the biggest hop growers.

The merger, for which Barrett Burston shareholders received some eighteen million Henry Jones shares, virtually doubled the size of the company, as the 1980 annual report spelled out: 'The issued capital of Henry Jones has increased from 27.9 million to 45.9 million shares; total assets employed have increased from $144 million to $222 million; shareholders' funds have been increased from $45.1 million to $84 million, and sales are expected to exceed $400 million in financial 1981.'[116]

The 1980 results were again a record. There were no inputs, of course, from Barrett Burston, as the deal was just being consummated. To 3 October, net operating profit after tax was $7.9 million ($13.4 million), a lift of 83 per cent, and shareholders' dividend was raised from 10 cents to 13.5 cents a share.[117]

All shareholders had good reason to feel warm about their investment, and the original management quartet was accumulating, as all good managements should be able to do, their own holdings: Elliott 311,055 beneficially held shares, Scanlon 147,156, Wiesener 109,924 and Cowper 94,376.[118] Naturally the excellent recovery from the dark days of the mid-1970s was not lost on the biggest shareholder, the CBA, whose Doug Stride had backed Elliott originally in the expectation of a quick killing. The bank's directors decided to grab their money and run. This meant that Henry Jones's chairman, Tim Marcus Clark, was obliged to resign. His natural successor came from the merger with Barrett Burston: Sir Ian McLennan. After retiring from the BHP chairmanship, McLennan had chaired the ANZ Banking Group and, then aged seventy-one, was in fine form. He was to prove himself again as a strong figure in deals that lay ahead. The restructuring of the board also afforded Richard Wiesener the chance to slip away. No doubt tired of commuting week after week from his home in Sydney, he had resigned his executive duties earlier; now, perhaps haunted by the death of his only son in a road accident while on a school expedition, he wanted to move to Monaco with his wife and two daughters and set up his own business.[119]

The exit of such a substantial shareholder as the CBA (and Elders GM went, too) exposed Elliott to takeover. So he did two things quickly: he reorganised the share structure, and he sought a friendly major investor. The reorganisation involved winding up the original holding company, GMH, which held 76 per cent of Henry Jones. By making the GMH shareholders direct holders of Henry Jones shares, he effectively diluted the CBA and Elders holdings as well as that of National Mutual (who stuck), so that upon their departure they could be replaced by a single investor holding about a third of Henry Jones.[120] But who? 'Carlton and United was the first group Mr Elliott thought of,' wrote Stephen Bartholomeusz in the *Age*.[121] And the brewery was more than willing. As Robert Gottliebsen explained, 'CUB knew it was vulnerable itself and the board, led by Sir Edward Cohen and John Madden Baillieu, knew they had to change if they were to survive. So, when Sir Edward and Lou Mangan sat down with Sir Ian and John Elliott and worked out a deal whereby CUB bought the CBA's and Elders' stakes in Henry Jones, it was as if the shackles were cut from Elliott's hands. CUB ended up with 33 per cent of Henry Jones.'[122]

The actual deal was done on-market and was extremely well orchestrated by the team. 'Within minutes of the stock exchange opening' on

Thursday, 4 December, fifteen million shares were traded by Potter Partners as 'CUB made its first move outside the brewing industry. . . . This valued Henry Jones at $123 million, or 16 per cent above the company's reorganised shareholders' funds.[123] John Baillieu recalls that he and Charles Goode, the senior partner at Potter's, really promoted the purchase inside the CUB board. It was his first meeting with Elliott, and it left an impression: 'I've met a few remarkable men, but none as remarkable as John Elliott. We've got on well from day one.'[124]

The two big deals of calendar 1980—the Barrett Burston merger and taking CUB as major shareholder—saw the board of Henry Jones blow out from nine to eighteen, a football team! But the company was clearly stronger; and the management team, with eight years of hard experience together, was in great shape for the next leap forward, the capture of Elders GM.

chapter **5**

The Birth of
Management
Takeovers

The rise and demise of Michael Robert Hamilton Holmes à Court as an entrepreneurial force in the 1970s and 1980s is a fascinating tale in itself, landmarked by the crash of October 1987 which led Elliott, with a good deal of justice, to dismiss the man as a paper shuffler.[1] By the later 1970s, this Africa-raised solicitor was starting to live out his British family motto, *Grandescunt aucta labore*—'Increased by work, they grow large'.[2] From a base purchase of a rundown textile operation, Western Australian Worsted and Woollen Mills, he had progressed to take over the substantial transport and engineering group Bell Brothers Holdings and had made his first impact in eastern Australia by playing a catalyst role in the play that saw the ageing Sir Reginald Ansett lose his airline to Rupert Murdoch and Sir Peter Abeles—a play that gave Holmes à Court and his shareholders a clear $11 million ($44 million). His languid wit and passion for collecting—pictures, expensive homes and Rolls-Royces (at one time he had seven of them, including the Silver Ghost Robert Redford drove in the film of *The Great Gatsby*)[3]—made him the darling of the financial press. His shrewd investments in likely target corporations made him the devil of directors who saw themselves as victims. To many in the money market, it looked as if Holmes à Court made raiding investments in a decidedly haphazard manner, an approach he has half refuted: 'We carry out no research and we do not seek investment opportunities. . . . The philosophy behind the companies we choose to buy shares in are companies with which we are familiar . . . companies that would fit in with our group.'[4]

Such a company was Elder Smith Goldsbrough Mort. Holmes à Court's first foray into Elders GM shares came over a fortnight in January 1980, when he started buying at $2.18 a share. When the price reached $3.50 on 1 February, he sold the lot—at a probable average

Robert Holmes à Court (courtesy of the Melbourne Herald).

profit of 30 per cent.[5] His second foray started in April 1980, when the price was $2.66. Most of the shares were bought by a subsidiary, Petroleum Distributors, and most were registered by brokers in their nominee companies, although Holmes à Court said later, 'None of our investments are secret and none of them are bought in nominee companies with the purpose of hiding the identity.'[6] By the end of 1980, Holmes à Court's holding in Elders GM had built to 2.6 million fully paid shares and 1 million partly paid—about 5.6 per cent of the capital.[7] (Interestingly, from the time he bought Bell Brothers six years earlier, Holmes à Court was a fifty-fifty partner with Elders in the general transport contractor Elder Bell Pty Ltd, operating out of Myaree

Veiled as the buying had been, secrets do not survive in the money market for long. Elders' manager in the west, Franciscus Bernardus (Frank) Bongers, picked up the mail before Christmas and reported it to his managing director, Charles Schmidt, not improving the holiday season for that emotionally inclined executive.[9] Further, Holmes à Court was not the only big player to be interested in Elders; Rupert Murdoch had identified the company as a cheap investment opportunity and, after discussions with his fellow chief executive of Ansett, Sir Peter Abeles, in which they agreed to act together, had instructed the broker Ord Minnett to buy up to a million shares to a top price of $3.25 a share. The first parcels of 164,850 fully paid shares and 189,300 contributing shares were secured at the end of 1980 in the name of a News Limited subsidiary, Startime of Australia, although they were registered under Beaglemoat Nominees, an Ord Minnett nominee company. Early in 1981 the Murdoch-Abeles holding was lifted to 851,000 shares, still under Beaglemoat, which caused consternation to both Holmes à Court and Schmidt.[10] The price, of course, rose in parallel with widespread market speculation.

Holmes à Court let it be known to the media late in January 1981 that Bell held about 7 per cent of Elders, but poured oil on troubled waters by telephoning Bongers and 'volunteering his personal undertaking . . . that there would be no substantial change in the Bell holding in Elders GM without Bell first consulting with Elders GM'.[11] During that conversation he described his holding as an 'investment', contradicting his own philosophy about investment opportunities.

Things bubbled along through February. At the Bell board meeting on the 25th, Holmes à Court proposed lifting the holding in Elders from 7 to 20 per cent, but it was decided to make no move until after Elders released the half-year results in a week's time. These duly showed a profit lift of nearly 13 per cent, and the share price responded with a rise of some 25 cents to $3.50. By now there was constant market buzz of a takeover, and some of the institutions were offering parcels of Elders shares to Holmes à Court. In three days early in March he picked up 500,000 shares from the AMP Society.

But Holmes à Court was not happy. On market, the mystery buyer was topping him. 'We did not know his identity,' he admitted. 'We did not know his objectives. We did not know whether he was friendly or unfriendly to our position.'[12] So, as Sir Norman Young recalls, 'without warning, the blow fell—on 18th March, 1981'.[13] Holmes à Court held an informal meeting of Bell directors in his office, and they decided to offer for 50 per cent of Elders capital at $4.00 a share. The mystery buyer was the first to respond, selling out that day to Holmes à Court; Murdoch and Abeles split a painless profit of more than a million dollars. Murdoch said later to Young (who was chairman of News Limited as well as chairman of Elders), 'I knew you would go straight to the government, and we would be locked into some damn thing because you would get a ten per cent limitation.'[14] He was right and wrong.

The very next day, Young went to see Roger Goldsworthy, the acting premier of South Australia, and Trevor Griffin, the attorney-general, seeking protection. He asked them to limit any holding, individual or group, in Elders to 10 per cent—the rule then applying to shareholdings in authorised banks and used earlier to protect other South Australian enterprises, including Santos and the South Australian Gas Company. He failed. 'They held the view that market forces should determine such issues and that it really was of no importance to the state who owned or controlled the principal South Australian business undertakings.'[15]

So the scene was set for a tempestuous ten days which would see everything from high drama to financial farce as Elders sought a saviour from the wild man of the west. In doing so, as Young has recalled, the company underwent 'unplanned and unwanted reconstruction which . . . destroyed its much-respected independence as one of South Australia's most influential business enterprises'.[16] Another view is that the outcome paved the way for a geriatric Goliath to be transformed into a global David. Here is how events unfolded:

In the strategy office of Henry Jones in Garden Street, South Yarra, Bob Cowper and Peter Scanlon had maintained a running file on Elders 'because it had a lot of characteristics in common with the old Henry Jones—very conservative'.[17] The file was on the top of the heap early in 1981 as Holmes à Court's action in Elders started to get publicity. A new entry went in on 11 February following a dinner party the night before at the Hilton Hotel for the original backers assembled by Elliott. Representing the Elders investment was Charles Faggotter, then an assistant general manager in the Adelaide office. Scanlon recalled: 'We asked him what Holmes à Court was up to. He said there was no problem; he played it down a bit too naively. So John [Elliott] rang Schmidt—because Elders were supporters of ours—and Schmidt said, "There's nothing to worry about." So there was nothing more for us to do at that time, but we kept the file handy.'[18]

(Scanlon explains that strategists like Cowper and himself get some of their information from annual reports, but other things are more revealing. They watch changes in shareholdings, whether or not they are in friendly hands. They keep an eye on property sales. They monitor the share price in relation to book values. They assess how conservative accounting practices might be. They read the financial pages carefully, monitoring executive appointments and keeping an eye out for statements by chief executives. 'If you collect them over time, you can usually tell what they think their problems are; they are over-defensive about them.' In a sentence: 'You are a company detective, always looking for clues.')[19]

While Elliott's strategists put Elders on hold, takeover speculation mounted. Then, on quite another matter, Scanlon lunched in Sydney with 'a good friend', Peter Charles Joseph, an enterprising financial consultant who was receiving a $1,000-a-month retainer from Henry Jones to advance certain issues in New South Wales.[20] 'I noticed that Peter talked a good deal about Elders,' Scanlon recalled. 'My ears pricked up a bit, and I made another note for the file.'[21]

In fact, Joseph was involved in one of the two sub-plots which made the battle for Elders so fascinating. It had become obvious, as Holmes à Court built his holding in Elders, that the target was looking for financial friends. At the same time a Sydney solicitor called John McGuigan was keen to sell his 45 per cent shareholding in White Industries, a coal miner in New South Wales and Queensland. Joseph, in concert with his close business friend Robert Alexander Ferguson, a director of BT Australia (a subsidiary of Bankers Trust New York Corporation), devised a plan (code-named Tulip) for Elders to buy all or part of McGuigan's parcel. This was being negotiated with Geoffrey Bernard White, chairman of White Industries, when Holmes à Court announced his takeover offer for Elders on 19 March 1981. That announcement raised the tempo, and over the next few days, while White was keen to help Elders, the defensive role shifted to BT Australia itself rather than White Industries.

The ever-watchful Scanlon traced Joseph to Coolangatta, on the Queensland Gold Coast, on the night of the takeover announcement and telephoned him. He recalled a conversation like this:

SCANLON: I noticed when we lunched that you seemed to have a lot of knowledge of the people at Elders. So I wonder if you are involved in defending them or helping them?

JOSEPH: I can't really tell you what I'm involved in there. But, yes, I do know them and I am working with them, not necessarily in a formal capacity.

SCANLON: Well, I'm just letting you know that we are interested in that company. We think there is a symmetry between ours and theirs. If there is something to be done, you ought not forget us.

JOSEPH: There is nothing at the moment. It's too early. But it might get out of hand.[22]

Friday, 20 March, saw solid trading in Elders shares on national share markets, despite suspension for two hours and twenty-nine minutes by the Adelaide exchange during the afternoon while some of the takeover terms were clarified. At the end of the day, Holmes à Court announced that his subsidiary Petroleum Distributors had lifted its holding in Elders to 7.7 million shares, or 12.4 per cent.[23] The weekend was fairly frantic, and a second sub-plot emerged: Peter Owens, the forceful managing director of Advertiser Newspapers, knocked on Sir Norman Young's front door and offered his company—as much a pillar of the Adelaide establishment as Elders—as a white knight. They talked for an hour or more, and Young has recalled, 'I told Peter Owens that I very much welcomed the unsolicited offer by the *Advertiser* to take up a significant buying role in the market. I also expressed the view that Elders shares were a good investment at $4.00.'[24] (Their discussions were interrupted when Young went to another room to take a call from the Elders men who were at that moment in Sydney talking details of the Tulip defence. Owens was not aware that any other party was involved in the saving of Elders.) Owens's chairman, Sir Arthur Rymill, telephoned Young that night to confirm that they would enter the market the following day to buy up to 9.9 per cent of the Elders capital.

Trading on Monday, 23 March, was furious, with both Holmes à Court and Owens going for every Elders share they could get. Deals opened at $4.05 a share, went to $4.10 within minutes, and were $4.22 before the first hour was out. At the close of trading they were $4.30.[25] Holmes à Court announced that Petroleum Distributors held ten million Elders shares, some 16 per cent. Newspaper reports put Owens's holding at under 3 per cent.

By then some curious changes were taking place. The plan for White Industries to buy the holding assembled by Holmes à Court fell apart because the price had grown too high; instead, BT Australia and Joseph took on the role of principal and had indeed telephoned Holmes à Court several times seeking to buy him out. At the same time, Owens apparently decided to go beyond the 9.9 per cent sanctioned by his board and instructed the brokers A. C. Goode & Co. to keep buying. He let it be known that some of his overseas friends were interested buyers. Meanwhile, Cowper and Scanlon watched and waited. On the Monday evening, Joseph called to tip off Scanlon that Schmidt of Elders would telephone the following morning.[26]

Trading on Tuesday, 24 March, was even more hectic. Holmes à Court raised his bid price to five dollars, and Owens instructed his brokers to top it. By early afternoon they held just on a third of Elders shares between them. Something had to give. Schmidt did duly telephone Scanlon that morning and asked him and Cowper to come to

Adelaide forthwith for talks with Sir Norman Young. Elliott himself had been overseas for more than a fortnight but was flying back. They caught the next plane.

During the two-and-a-half hour meeting, Young outlined his rather grandiose plan, which was that given Holmes à Court would be repulsed, a holding company would buy all the shares in Elders, Carlton and United Breweries, South Australian Breweries and Henry Jones, and each company would continue to conduct its own business under the protective umbrella of the holding company.[27] This had no appeal for Scanlon and Cowper and was soon abandoned. Young then asked them to prepare a proposition which would be of assistance to Elders, and they said they would within three days. Scanlon recalled, 'When Bob and I went to Elders it was not the words but the vibes which were so clear. It was quite clear that they were under pressure. They kept asking us questions about the ownership of shares in terms of section 129 of the Companies Act which concerns a company buying its own shares. This obviously concerned their dealing with Peter Joseph and BT Australia, although they gave no details, just asked questions.'[28] (Scanlon makes the point that there should always be a negotiating team of two; one to do the talking, the other to observe. 'Half of what you are telling me is not in your words,' he says, 'but in your eyes, the way you are looking at your companions. To determine whether the other side are anxious sellers or willing sellers or not sellers at all is all that matters. Interpretations are critical if you are going to come out and instruct your team correctly. I always have someone with me, someone to check the vibes.')[29]

Towards the end of the Adelaide meeting, Schmidt rushed into the room exclaiming, 'We've saved her. We've saved Elders.'[30] He had just heard that Holmes à Court had abandoned his takeover and sold his holding, just on 20 per cent, to BT Australia at $5.10 a share, giving him a profit from the exercise of $16.5 million ($26.4 million)—and because the transaction was actually the sale of Petroleum Distributors, whose only assets were the Elders shares, it escaped tax. Why did Holmes à Court cut and run? 'There were two other parties [BT Australia and Owens],' he said later, 'who could, in a very short space of time, hold 40 per cent of the capital of Elders and have interests different from ours. That situation was potentially going to become very disadvantageous to us.'[31]

Holmes à Court's surprise exit did not solve Elders' problems; it simply complicated them. For BT Australia had bought his parcel in the firm belief that Elders could on-sell the shares—hence the questions about section 129. And Owens's 18 per cent holding was in limbo, or at least a mystery. This enabled Scanlon and Cowper to leave Adelaide in a somewhat ebullient mood. 'They were definitely under substantial pressure,' said Scanlon, 'and therefore we could put a proposition which was much tougher than we may otherwise have been able to do.'[32] He added, 'My reading of the situation was that Elders had told BT Australia that they had a buyer and asked BT to act on their behalf; and then, when they had acted, Elders had trouble delivering the buyer. BT were very annoyed with Elders. They had been put on the spot.'[33]

Scanlon and Cowper worked overnight at Garden Street preparing the proposition to discuss with Elliott when he came straight from the airport on arrival back from overseas on Wednesday, 25 March. By lunchtime the three had agreed on the proposal to be put to Elders. It was for a reverse takeover in which Elders would appear to buy Henry Jones but the Elliott team would run the new and expanded company—not only a reverse takeover but a management takeover! Briefly, the terms were: Elders would make a takeover bid for Henry Jones on the basis of one one-dollar share in Elders for each fifty-cent share in Henry Jones, with Henry Jones shareholders who did not want Elders shares to receive $4.40 a share in cash; Henry Jones or an associate would buy the Holmes à Court parcel of 20 per cent of Elders shares then held by BT Australia, and the board of Elders would reflect the new ownership, with Sir Ian McLennan as chairman and Elliott as chief executive.[34] Elliott outlined this proposal to Young on the telephone that afternoon, and it was agreed that an Elders team led by Schmidt would attend Garden Street the next day to discuss the proposition. Young, however, still entertained hopes for his grand plan under a holding company, but these were dashed in a short meeting with Lou Mangan, the chief executive at Carlton and United and a director of Henry Jones. He liked the idea as little as Scanlon and Cowper had.

The Elders team plus Peter Joseph met with Scanlon at Garden Street. Elliott was over at the breweries' headquarters in Bouverie Street, which was probably just as well, as there had been antipathy between him and Schmidt previously,[35] and they were now on a collision course. In fact, the Bouverie Street meeting was the more important of the two, because Elliott had to convince his biggest shareholder that the reverse takeover was a sound plan.[36] Further, he had to place Petroleum Distributors, which was a hot potato burning BT Australia's fingers. Elliott recalled, 'Those shares were in limbo. I said that we would buy them but that it would be better if the brewery bought them. John Baillieu, a key Carlton director, said, "Yes, we'll do it." That was crucial.'[37] The Garden Street meeting was really a lay-down misère; the Elders team could not take a trick because Scanlon told them the plan was not negotiable. Schmidt telephoned Elliott from the airport in an attempt to settle his own future. Elliott said the chief executive question would be a matter for their respective chairmen, but he expected to get it.[38]

The boards of both Elders and Henry Jones held meetings on Friday, 27 March. The Henry Jones board quickly approved the terms of the merger put to Elders, and then Elliott and Sir Ian McLennan spent the rest of the day fielding questions on the telephone from Young. For the Elders directors' meeting was long and agonising. While they approved the financial terms—subject to Charles Faggotter flying to Melbourne to check some of the Henry Jones projections—they were not happy about the proposed composition of the new board. Four out of nine of them, including Young and Schmidt, would lose their seats (interestingly, these directors held just .03 per cent of their company's issued capital, exercising power without personal risk).[39] And they did not relish the idea of McLennan and Elliott being chairman and chief executive. After several hours they adjourned, pending a face-to-face confrontation between Young and McLennan and Elliott. That night, the Henry Jones camp 'doubted whether the merger would go ahead',[40] but they did not know how Young was thinking. 'By this time I was satisfied that, broadly speaking, the Henry Jones proposal was one that was fair and reasonable to Elders' shareholders,' Young said later. 'I considered that the Henry Jones top management was more innovative than that of Elders.'[41]

Young flew alone to Melbourne on Sunday, 29 March, aware that his managing director was in something of a mess. At four o'clock he met with Elliott and McLennan at the stately Windsor Hotel, originally a temperance coffee house but in this century a home-from-home for Western District graziers. It was a sticky meeting from the outset, Elliott and McLennan reiterating that the proposals were not negotiable, Young arguing against Henry Jones 'nominating the chairman and chief executive, particularly as Elders was the bigger company'.[42] He made no progress, and Elliott recalls that Sir Ian was 'wonderfully strong'. Young wrote later in his memoirs, 'McLennan, who was then 72 years of age and had already been required to retire previously from the chairmanship of BHP and the ANZ Bank because he had reached the retiring age for directors of these two companies, insisted that it was a vital element of the merger that he be chairman and that the Articles (which said the chairman must retire at 70) would have to be altered.' Then, in a burst of passion untypical of this wry Scot, Young wrote, 'What a strange combination of conceit and blind self-interest was to be observed in McLennan's demand.'[43] McLennan has strongly refuted this: 'It wasn't my demand that I become chairman, it was the demand of the Henry Jones board; they wanted the team of Elliott and McLennan to go on. The other thing was that it is essential that the chairman and managing director be very compatible and live in the same place, Melbourne. There was no self-interest as far as I was concerned.'[44]

Young flew home empty-handed, and that night the adjourned meeting of the Elders board was resumed. The directors, having no real alternative, accepted the draft press release that Elliott and his team had prepared, which spelled out the terms of what was a management takeover. It was released the next day and stated in part:

> The directors of both companies are confident of the benefits to shareholders of the merged group. The merged group will: under normal trading conditions pay a dividend of at least 25 cents per share per annum; have assets which, on a conservative basis, total over $1 billion; have turnover in excess of $2.5 billion; be one of the largest Australian companies with the necessary financial strength to support further growth. . . .
>
> It has been agreed that the Board of Elders will be re-organised with five existing Elders directors and five directors from Henry Jones. At that time, Mr John D. Elliott will become Chief Executive Officer of the merged group. The existing Chairman of Elders, Sir Norman Young, will retire from that office at the end of this year in accordance with the Company's Articles.
>
> Elders have invited Sir Ian McLennan, Chairman of Henry Jones, and Mr John D. Elliott, Managing Director of Henry Jones, to join the Board of Elders immediately.[45]

This was the start of a huge leap forward for both companies, and it was a singular development in Australian takeovers. Young still maintains, 'I have always regarded the events of 1981 as a merger in the true sense. Elders was the significant company and it was appointed to become the shareholders' flagship. It was Elders first—Elders IXL.'[46] But Geoff Lord, now boss of Elders Resources, remembers it differently: 'The first real break came when Elders were in trouble and we were able to back-door Henry Jones in there. They saw it as a merger. But it was actually a management takeover—the management team runs the expanded vehicle.'[47]

Indeed, it was a big expansion for the management team. From issued capital of $14 million and net assets of $33 million in the parent Henry Jones, their bailiwick leapt more than tenfold by 1982 to issued capital of $162 million and net assets of $348 million in the revamped Elders IXL.[48] The rollcall of subsidiary companies exploded from 36 in five countries, with a book value of $49 million, to 307 in fourteen countries, with a book value of $308 million. The new emphasis was on pastoral business through more than three hundred stock-and-station branches in all states; the company handled one in every three bales of wool sold at auction. But finance and merchant banking and steel and metals distribution were important, too.

The new board of directors did not line up quite as forecast in the takeover announcement. McLennan and Elliott did, indeed, join the Elders board at once, and 'amicable relations' were established.[49] (Elliott recalls that one early meeting was not all that amicable as far as he was concerned. It was held on Melbourne Cup day, which is a holiday in Victoria but not in South Australia. The night before, Elliott attended, as he has now for twenty-four years, a Calcutta sweep dinner with a hundred mates from school and university days, many of whom he sees only that once a year. His table secured a horse called Just a Dash, to be ridden in the Cup by Peter Cook. The party broke up at two in the morning, and Elliott had to catch the first flight to Adelaide. Over lunch the directors organised a modest sweep, and the woman who had prepared the lunch drew Just a Dash. There was much excitement when Just a Dash won and the woman collected her ten dollars. 'I had to sit there, knowing that my mates were celebrating our twenty-thousand-dollar win and I was missing out!'[50])

Before the new board could be finalised, a couple of problems had to be sorted out. When Elders bought Henry Jones in the reverse take-over, the CUB holding was diluted from around 32 per cent of Henry Jones to 10 or 12 per cent of Elders and the new entity was open again to another takeover raid by Holmes à Court, a move he was known to be contemplating. Further, there were still considerable parcels of shares floating about, including the extra ones bought under instructions from Owens. So, to restore its position, CUB made a partial take-over bid of its own. Shares flooded to it, and at one time the brewery held more than 50 per cent. But its sharebroker, Charles Goode, kept a close eye on things, and the final result was the one desired: 49.444 per cent.[51] In the end, the new Elders IXL board numbered eighteen instead of ten. Five continued from the old Elders GM board: Des Chenery, the general manager of pastoral activities who had been with the company more than forty years; Alan McGregor, a lawyer and company director; Ian McLachlan, a grazier soon to be the most successful president of the National Farmers' Federation; Gerald Niall, a barrister and solicitor and long-time director of heavy companies, including National Mutual and the ANZ Banking Group; and Joseph Winter, an accountant and chairman of Adsteam and SA Brewing who had a number of other directorships. Seven were from the old Henry Jones board: McLennan, Elliott, Bails Myer, Stephen Kimpton, E. A. (Ted) Burton—the second National Mutual man on the new board—Scanlon and Cowper. (Bob Cowper did not stay long; after ten years on the Elliott team, he decided to go and join Wiesener in Monaco. Both continued their association from afar and were to play important parts in later developments.) And six came from the biggest shareholder, CUB: John Baillieu, the sharebroker; David Darling, former head prefect and captain of cricket at Geelong Grammar and a shrewd investor; David Hegland, an American who flew planes off US aircraft-carriers during World War II and later bossed General Motors-Holden's; Tony Macdougall, whose Sands & Macdougall printed most of CUB's labels; and Lou Mangan.[52] Of that original Elders IXL board, half still serve today (1988) and, in line with an ongoing Elliott policy, have been joined by five senior executives: Peter Bartels, Ken Biggins, Ken Jarrett, Geoff Lord and Michael Nugent.

(Fascinating postscripts to the Elders takeover were written by John William von Doussa—then, at forty, a Queen's Counsel and vice-president of the Law Society of South Australia—who was appointed in May 1981 by the state minister for corporate affairs, Trevor Griffin, as an inspector to investigate dealings in the shares of Elders GM and Petroleum Distributors between 1 January and 25 May 1981.[53] His report covered 312 pages, plus a third again in appendixes. The most intriguing passages concern the hapless Peter Owens of the *Advertiser*, who sought out Sir Norman Young to offer his company's support. Von Doussa reveals that when the actual deal was done, 'Owens had received no forewarning of the merger',[54] which was no way for Young to treat a would-be rescuer, but that is beside the point. The interesting focus was upon the mystery overseas buyers for whom Owens bought shares after his original, authorised 9.9 per cent were secured. He told von Doussa that he had made phone calls to them, but the inspector-sleuth was ahead of him: 'At my request the computer records in relation to the telephone service to Owens' home have been checked. There is no record of any overseas calls.'[55] In the end, von Doussa called upon Owens to identify the buyers. He refused, 'saying that he felt bound by his undertaking to maintain their anonymity'. This was legally contemptuous, and after more than a year of toing and froing in courts, Owens was 'committed to prison for contempt by the Full Supreme Court of South Australia'. He served seventy-one days in jail. He was further fined eleven hundred dollars for three breaches concerning share dealings. And he was fired by Advertiser Newspapers. Von Doussa concluded: 'Owens received no instructions from overseas corporations . . . his story to the contrary is false.'[56] In a commercial drama in which most parties came out even or ahead, Owens was the heavy loser.)

The new team bedded down Elders IXL, lifting net operating profit in their first full year, 1981–82, by 78 per cent to $61.3 million and by a further 5 per cent in 1982–83 to $64.3 million, despite the worst drought in Australian pastoral history.[57] During this time, Elliott and Scanlon turned their attention once again to a company called Wood Hall. It had appealed to them before the Elders drama intervened, and over months they had built a holding of 4.9 per cent in the parent English company, Wood Hall Trust. This company had been put together over thirty years by Michael Richards, a lawyer-turned-merchant-banker and as needle-witted as only Yorkshiremen are among the English. It was a conglomerate with all sorts of tempting Australian goodies. The jewel in the crown was the former Australian Mercantile Land and Finance Company (AML & F), a pastoral house with traditions going back almost as far as Elder Smith's and which embraced the

David Darling — joined the Elders board from the brewery.

lesser, but equally old, wool-broking firms of Dennys Lascelles and Strachan & Co., who handled much of the Western District clip going out through the port of Geelong, and the Australian Estates Co. Also valuable was the Hornibrook construction group, which worked on major contracts throughout Australia, Papua New Guinea and Fiji. Additionally, Wood Hall owned the long-established trading houses Paterson Simons & Co. and M. D. Ewart & Co., which operated right through the Far East, Africa, Europe and Britain, and Haven Automation, which specialised in marine, offshore and land-based automation and control systems in Singapore, Malaysia, the Philippines and Hong Kong, as well as being a joint venturer in the People's Republic of China. The Elders takeover made Wood Hall even more appealing. Elliott recalled, 'It was strategically sensible, as Elders had thirty-five per cent of the pastoral business and Wood Hall had another fifteen.'[58]

Having done their homework, Elliott and Scanlon flew to London to manage a dawn raid on Wood Hall. The day was Tuesday, 9 February 1982. 'We had eight brokers going for their lives from eight-thirty in the morning, phoning institutions,' Elliott recalled. 'By ten a.m. it was all over—and half the fellows hadn't even reached the City.' (Indeed, the brokers were doubly confounded by a railway strike!) 'We finished up with twelve per cent and rang Richards, who was getting old and a bit tired, and said we'd like to have a talk. We negotiated from a position of strength.'[59] Elliott announced that Richards had accepted a $90 million bid for the company. (The dawn raid was an accepted strategem in the City of London, with its own rules. But the brokers were so outraged by the thrust of the two then-unknown Australians that the rules were changed within a week. Henceforth, Elliott said, 'no raids could start before nine-thirty a.m.',[60] to give the bowler-hat brigade ample time to get in from the stockbroker belt in the Home Counties!) The purchase of Wood Hall, and with it the AML & F network, gave Elders Pastoral nearly five hundred branches throughout rural Australia with a staff of more than four thousand. It was far and away the biggest stock-and-station group ever seen in Australia, and it handled just on one in every two bales of wool to go through the auction system.[61]

Elliott and his team moved in a new direction, too, in 1982. They bought 19.8 per cent of the issued share capital of Bridge Oil, a partner in the Cooper Basin consortium in South Australia supplying natural gas to Sydney and Adelaide and also a partner in the Surat Basin supplying gas to Brisbane. Bridge was also an aggressive oil, diamonds and minerals explorer, and it soon bought 14.8 per cent of Santos, the biggest partner in the Cooper Basin. The Bridge investment cost Elders nearly $20 million, and Elliott and Scanlon joined its board. In a very different investment, Peter Bartels and Michael Nugent went to China for the inauguration of Nanning Jones, a joint venture with the People's Republic of China to grow pineapples at Nanning.[62]

Peter Bartels — carried the Elders flag into China.

Payments for these enterprises were helped by the treasure of disposable assets the management team discovered when they took over Elders. Elliott talked to finance reporters about selling off redundant assets worth $100 million.[63] He sold off, too, the last of the difficult deciduous fruit operations which had been at the heart of the original Henry Jones. 'The company withdrew from the Australian canned-fruit industry on satisfactory terms. This decision was taken because of the need for rationalisation of production and marketing caused by the continued decline of export markets and worsening profitability.'[64] After ten years of battling, it must have been a mighty relief.

Altogether different was the year 1983, although expansion continued. Geoff Lord has identified what he calls Elliott's strong skills: 'He's a good front man because of his enormous strength. When he makes up his mind that he is going to do something, he is very hard to stop. Secondly, he is very quick to organise structures, and he pulls you up with him.'[65] By 1983 he had structured Elders into five operational groups, each of which made remarkably similar contributions to the company's net income: Pastoral, which looked after wool broking, livestock selling, rural financing, real estate, insurance and merchandising; International, which traded all kinds of commodities, notably wool, all over the world and looked after shipping and ship chartering; Finance, which handled, through Elders finance, all aspects of merchant banking and, through Elders Lensworth Finance, property finance and leasing, as well as rural financing and investment management; Materials, which ranged from hops and malt for brewing and timber and building supplies through to metals, mining and construction; and Food, which grew or processed margarine, frozen foods, pineapples, grain-fed beef and animal feeds and retailed wine and spirits.

But the year had non-business developments. Elliott—who, with Gordon Darling, had induced Tony Eggleton to return from the Commonwealth Secretariat in London to become federal director of the Liberal Party in 1975[66]—planned Liberal strategy in Victoria for Malcolm Fraser's last election campaign in the spring of 1983, as he had done for Fraser's successful campaigns in 1975, 1977 and 1980. ('I always found Malcolm hard work,' he recalled. 'It was always an amicable and cordial relationship, although in debate on ideas he always berated you and went for you, and then sometime later you'd see him doing things you had suggested.'[67]) The 1983 campaign was a disaster, and Hawke became Labor's new prime minister. It left the Liberal Party in Victoria with badly bruised finances, and something had to be done. At a finance committee meeting attended by Elliott, John Calvert-Jones (the stockbroker now in charge of Prudential Bache in Australia), Richard Pratt (the packaging multimillionaire) and Elliott's long-time stockbroking friend Peter Lawrence, the idea was adopted to launch the '500 Club' for five hundred Liberal supporters who would each contribute five hundred dollars a year to Liberal funds in return for entertaining functions with party leaders. 'It is the biggest contributor to the party,' Elliott has stated. 'I got the first two hundred and fifty members by going round the Melbourne business community. I knew them all. Then I came to a grinding halt. The guy who built it up to five hundred was Julian Beale, assisted by Jenny Emanuel.' (Julian Howard Beale, MHR for the suburban seat of Deakin and a shadow minister, the son of a former Australian Ambassador to Washington and a Harvard MBA, made his fortune out of Moonie Oil; he attracted massive publicity in 1988 when he got into a contretemps over quarantine regulations after visiting Venezuela, a yellow-fever country in South America.) 'The fact was that all the business community sat on boards of directors and were not giving any money personally because their companies were contributing and they were satisfied in their own minds that they were doing their bit. I talked to them all—fellows like Jim Balderstone at BHP—and said, "What are you doing? We want you to join the 500 Club. It's only five hundred bucks." That got them in.'[68] (Smaller regional groups, like the 200 Club in Bendigo, have developed to swell the party coffers.)

That year, too, Elliott became president of the Carlton Football Club, head-hunted by former player and club eminence Laurie Kerr. 'I was offered the job before Ian Rice got it in 1980,' said Elliott, 'but I was too busy with the business.'[69] Elliott had once hoped to play for Carlton. Instead, he played 247 games for Carey Old Boys, for several seasons as captain. At Carlton he has lifted marketing and sponsorships and developed a lunching-and-watching club, the President's Men, which attracts top businessmen at an annual subscription that works out at rather more than a thousand dollars a game for the eleven matches each season that Carlton plays at Prince's Park. Lou Richards, the clown who lightens many of Elliott's luncheons, has said, 'The only bank that ain't here is the Blood Bank.'[70] An enthusiastic member who supplies office furniture told *Australian Business*'s Charles Wright, 'Our president is John Elliott and his philosophy is that he brings business people together and encourages them to trade fairly and hard with each other. He tells us: "Gentlemen, we are here to enjoy the footy, to support Carlton, vote Liberal, and do business with each other. If you support each other, you'll support Carlton." '[71] Such friends as Peter Lawrence, John McIntosh, Dick Pratt, Sam Smorgan and Will Bailey of the ANZ say, 'Hear, hear.'

Back to business, a bold acquisition was the purchase of the Commercial Bureau, the only Australian company with an accredited office in Moscow giving trading access to all of the Eastern Bloc in Europe. Elliott said at the time, 'We believe that if Australia is going to sell agricultural products this is one of the major markets they have to be sold in.'[72] The bureau has no monopoly in Russo-Australian trade, but under renewable three-year agreements, the latest signed in 1987, they agree to buy wool from Elders, and by way of barter, Elders buys white goods worth about $8 million a year from the Soviets, selling them in Australia under the Lemair brand. This contra trade is not in balance. The Russians take about ten thousand tonnes of wool a year from Elders which, at about ten dollars a kilogramme, is worth a gross of some $100 million in 1988.[73] The bureau also sells very substantial quantities of meat, grain and dairy products through its Moscow office, which is staffed by two expatriates—a permanent Australian and visiting Elders traders—and eight or nine Russians. The office acts as representative in Russia of BHP and Comalco as well as other Australian and European companies.[74]

At home, the executives were able at last to quit the cramped offices over a garage at 20 Garden Street, South Yarra. They moved across the road into splendidly refurbished premises above the shops in the Jam Factory. This is actually a huge expanse of floor, and parts of it had been prepared for Elders staff since 1981, the architectural work being done by partners Graham Whitford and Michael Peck—Whitford & Peck of Albert Park. (As a glimpse into business relationships, Whitford and Bob Cowper played together in the Victorian Sheffield Shield team, and the Peck and Elliott families are friends. The firm's speciality is community centres—including the one at Eltham, which is the biggest mud-brick building in the Southern Hemisphere, and the award-winning one at Mt Eliza—but they have done some seventy projects for Elders, including the Elders Investments office in Hong Kong.)[75] Executive offices and board and conference rooms are in Area One (there are five areas in all), a beautiful inner sanctum behind huge double timber doors. It has its own spacious reception area dominated by two spectacular outback paintings by Kenneth Jack: *Urandangi*

Area One interior.

(120 cm × 186 cm), a property in Queensland formerly owned by AML & F, and *Sunrise—Drought Country* (164 cm × 273 cm). The offices themselves display some lovely paintings: Drysdales, Boyds, Sir Arthur Streeton's evocative *Coogee* and, in Elliott's own office, a super impressionistic oil of the Sydney Opera House painted by Sir William Dobell in 1969 when he was seventy. (When the Elders Collection, which stems mainly from pre-takeover days, is sent interstate each year for a short season on tour in the care of its curator, Pamela Lewers, the walls suddenly look austere.)[76] Great pains have been taken with the furnishings. Whitford and Peck used photographs of the original Henry Jones board table in Hobart to get an exact replica in Huon Pine, and interior decorator John Coote (one of the President's Men at Carlton) was called in to do the colour scheme in Elliott's office and advise on the carpeting throughout.[77] In these days when image is considered important, the Area One complex radiates one word: *success.*

Yet the biggest success of 1983 came in the last month, a pre-Christmas present of sensational dimensions, even if it did cost the best part of a billion dollars.[78]

chapter 6
The Beer Barrel Polka

Of the four significant takeover masters on the Australian scene—Elliott, Holmes à Court, Bond and Brierley—only Elliott is Australian-born. Holmes à Court, as we have seen, came out of Africa. Alan Bond was born in London, almost within earshot of Bow Bells. And Ronald Alfred Brierley was born and grew up in Wellington, New Zealand. The competitive compulsions of the four, and the comparative smallness of the local business community, meant that they were bound to clash. Further, they are all of an age—only four years spans their birthdays—and they emerged as market forces at much the same time. In round one, Holmes à Court threw the first punch, but Elliott won Elders. In round two, only a skirmish, Holmes à Court again struck first, spending some $10 million on a 2-to-3 per cent stake in Carlton and United in April 1982. It was probably his second go at Elders, because CUB was such a big shareholder. But Elliott bought him out immediately. 'It taught Holmes à Court that if he touched Elliott's kingdom, Elliott would try to move quickly to buy him out.'[1] In round three, the biggest corporate bout to that time in Australia, Brierley opened hostilities, but Elliott again came away with the crown.

Brierley (now Sir Ronald and a financial friend of the richest Australian, Kerry Packer) went to Wellington College and studied accountancy—and failed![2] When he was nineteen, he sold his stamp collection to finance a monthly newsletter in which he tipped shares. From his subscribers he raised some seventy thousand dollars to launch Brierley Investments Limited (BIL), his advertisements offering 'real adventure in the stockmarket'. (A thousand dollars invested originally in BIL was worth more than nine million dollars before the crash of 1987).[3] In the early 1960s, when he was twenty-six, Brierley moved across the Tasman to Sydney and made a modest home in the Crest Hotel at Kings Cross.[4] Soon after, he bought the failing Industrial Equity Limited (IEL) with $200,000 of his BIL money and turned it into an asset-stripping raider;[5] he was accused in the New South Wales Parlia-

Sir Ron Brierley (courtesy of the Melbourne Herald).

ment in 1979 of 'raping the assets' of his takeover targets. In private life, Brierley, a bachelor, has a passion for watching first-class cricket matches that matches Elliott's passion for football, and he has returned to his childhood favourite, a valuable stamp collection.[6]

At the end of November 1983, having quietly bought up some ten million shares in CUB, Brierley wrote to the chairman, Sir Edward Cohen, saying that he intended to buy another fifty million at $3.30 a share to take 'our holding to 60.34 million shares, which represents 23.91 per cent of the issued capital'.[7] The story broke on the morning of 30 November. Barbara A'Beckett, Elliott's eyes and ears for the considerable part of each year that he spends abroad, immediately started chasing him. She knew that he was flying from New York to San Francisco with Ken Jarrett, planning to overnight with an old McKinsey mate, Bill Spencer, so she left messages for him at Spencer's home. By the time they arrived there, it was too late to get an onward flight that day to Australia. Elliott was, of course, fully knowledgeable on CUB and aware that Elders and his own career were vulnerable to takeover by way of the brewery; indeed, he had discussed the threat with CUB directors.[8]

Having booked airplane seats for the next day, he and Jarrett got down to the figures while Scanlon and the team worked in Melbourne. 'We decided the best thing to do was buy CUB,' Elliott recalled. 'We knew it wouldn't be a very happy or friendly time.' He and Jarrett duly boarded a Pan-Am flight but learned that it was to be delayed for some hours. So Elliott raced to the Qantas desk while Jarrett tried to recover their baggage. The Qantas flight was headed for Townsville via Hawaii, and Elliott said they would go to Hawaii and try to get a Melbourne-bound plane from there. 'But Qantas said the list was closed and they could not take us because there would not be enough food on board! In the end they did hold the plane and we took off; but we had no luck at Hawaii and had to go on to Townsville where we chartered a jet to Melbourne.'[9]

Brierley savoured the sensation he had caused. He had shown that a giant which was considered impregnable was as much at risk as any other company in these takeover times. The normally shy little fellow with bat ears agreed to meet reporters, nominating the Cricketers' Bar at the Windsor Hotel as the venue. There he said he wanted to 'tidy up' CUB's share structure and intimated that he would sell off its investment in Elders.[10] In response to a question on his investment style, he said, 'Conservative. Logical, I hope. A realist rather than a pie-in-the-sky type.'[11] CUB shares that day closed 14 per cent higher at $3.55. That night a terse statement was issued from CUB's Bouverie Street fortress: 'There is a normal board meeting tomorrow. The board will decide if any comment is due to be made.'[12] Following that meeting, the directors issued a scornful communiqué: 'Shareholders can hardly be expected to take seriously a partial offer pitched so closely to prevailing market price.'[13]

Elliott and Jarrett arrived back in Melbourne for a hectic weekend. They worked with Scanlon and Sir Ian McLennan on an analysis to be presented at a meeting of the Elders board on the Sunday, a day the *Age*'s finance editor, Terry McCrann, designated 'Sunday, bloody Sunday'.[14] The board meeting was indeed painful, for six of the sixteen directors were also directors of CUB and were torn asunder. Of the five options canvassed, the one that appealed to them was an umbrella arrangement under which Elders would own 49 per cent of CUB just as CUB owned 49 per cent of Elders, thus protecting each other and continuing to function as separate businesses. But Elliott said it would not work. 'The irrefutable logic showed it was not in Elders best interest,' he recalls. 'Too much money locked up. Sir Ian was very strong. He told the CUB directors of their legal responsibility: while sitting at the Elders board they were obliged to act only in Elders' interest. . . . After considerable discussion, Sir Ian suggested the CUB blokes might like to talk among themselves. They went out of the room, and then he was very supportive of Scanlon and me. You see, a lot of our group had recently come out of Elders GM and were not really Henry Jones-type people. But to a man they became unanimous that we had to go to a hundred per cent of CUB. . . . When the CUB directors returned to the meeting, Sir Ian told them of our decision, and John Baillieu, who is a very good man, could see it was all over.'[15] The offer was: six Elders shares plus $12.20 for every ten CUB shares, a total bid of some $972 million, which valued the CUB shares at $3.86 each, although the cash required was only some $290 million with another $100 million for immediate on-market buying.[16]

John Baillieu — a wise head in a crisis.

The CUB directors then motored from Garden Street to Bouverie Street to tell their other fellow directors what was going on. They had the obvious option of going from 49 per cent to control of Elders, and that would have been that. (It was actually not so simple. A recently launched Elders IXL Employees Share Incentive Plan, designed to encourage the staff to become shareholders, had watered the CUB holding to some 47 per cent, and even if they bought the necessary 3 per cent, there was nothing to prevent Elliott and his colleagues from issuing more issues.) They did not do it. Indeed, the CUB directors copped a lot of flak for appearing to do nothing at all. The *Age* in its business awards for 1983 decreed, 'To the board of directors of CUB, the stunned mullet award for inertia in the face of crisis.'[17] In fact, control was never an option. As Baillieu recalled, 'There was not one man on the CUB board who was prepared to do that. It was never really an option. The managerial skill to run Elders was simply not there. We didn't have the expertise to handle it. And I don't think you could have assumed that Elliott's team would have stayed on.'[18]

Monday, 5 December, saw the brokers for Elders and IEL competing for CUB shares on the market, pushing the price from $3.65 to $3.80. Elliott spent about $60 million, and at the end of the day it was thought that he and Brierley each had about 9 per cent of CUB. That night Elliott contacted the raider, making an offer for his shares. It was explained that he would keep buying in the market, and if Brierley did not sell now he would miss out because later his parcel would push Elliott beyond the permitted 20 per cent limit without formal Part A documents having been sent to shareholders. Brierley had the night to think about it.[19] He did indeed phone back in the morning, selling to Elliott at $3.82 a share and showing a tidy profit on the week of between $8 million and $10 million.[20] It was a boost for Elliott, but it was not enough.

'By Wednesday we realised the thing would go on for a long time because we were offering paper,' he told Keith Dunstan later. 'I realised we had to get a cash bid, so along with other senior guys, we worked day and night for forty-eight hours and we got $750 million.'[21] This astonishing money raising in such a short time stunned everybody, particularly the CUB directors. But Ken Jarrett has explained the logic behind it:

> People say we did it in forty-eight hours, which is rubbish. For three years prior to that we had been talking to banks about what we were doing and developing a track record for paying back money when or before we said we would. So it didn't hit them as a surprise. And, although they came to tentative agreements within forty-eight hours, there were weeks of legal documentation and stuff like that. Certainly it was more than we had raised before. But size is not the problem in raising money; it's making sure that the banks are comfortable. The banks need to understand your business and feel happy about what you are doing. With CUB we could explain that it was a very strong cash-flow business; that on the asset values it seemed to be underpriced, and that we could free up a lot of assets—breweries which were not being used, warehouses and things like that—to repay the debt.[22]

The banks that came to the party were first the Hong Kong and Shanghai Banking Corporation, whose chief executive, William Purves, just happened to be in Australia visiting its daughter merchant bank, Wardley Australia Limited. Elliott told him what they wanted to do, and he gave his approval on the Thursday morning. Then, with the Hong Kong Bank in, Elliott was able to say to Citibank and Chase, 'You had better tell me quick-smart or I will go to someone else.'[23] The Elders board approved the cash plan on the Friday, just three minutes before the market opened, although the CUB members were suitably stunned. But that day saw a hitch: the Reserve Bank of Australia clapped a ban on all foreign-currency transactions because of the possible impact on the dollar of Elders' application to bring $700 million into the country. Elliott recalled, 'They had to make a decision. Luckily they opted to free the currency and we were able to bring it all in.'[24] Elders lifted its holding in CUB to 37 per cent on the Friday and by midday on Monday, 12 December, had won control. Buying was halted at 58 per cent and the offer left to run on. It was a splendid short, sharp campaign which signalled a completely new culture for the company; from a dominant pastoral house within Australia it was to become a global trader—a beer-led revolution!

But there was an expensive hiccup. To reap the benefit of the breweries' cash flow, it was necessary to get CUB delisted from the exchange, and this required a holding of more than 90 per cent so that outstanding shares could be acquired compulsorily. But a mystery buyer moved into the market after Christmas and operated through January and into February. This was Tan Chin Tuan, an old Chinese who had made a vast fortune in Singapore after spending the World War II years in Australia. Early in 1983 he had made an investment in 4 per cent of CUB's shares and was well known to its board. Possibly encouraged by some CUB directors who were not pleased to lose their power and position to Elders, Tan built his holding to more than 10 per cent, frustrating Elliott. After Elliott and Scanlon had made many visits to Singapore to identify the pest, they met face to face. 'He kept asking us to raise the bid,' Elliott recalled, 'and we said we wouldn't.'[25] In the end they had to, paying Tan a hefty $4.56 a share—a bonus of 74 cents above the offer price which cost Elders an extra $32 million. But it meant that their control was complete.

Elliott's stewardship of Elders' new subsidiary was in sharp contrast to his actions when he took control of Elders GM; then he had moved his own team into key posts and they had run the company, transferring headquarters to Garden Street. With the breweries he was much more gentle. Certainly the parent board was adjusted. Former Carlton directors Hegland, Macdougall and McKenzie departed. Their colleagues Baillieu (by then a deputy chairman of Elders), Darling and Mangan stayed on, joined by the breweries' number-two man, Fred Coulstock. Ken Jarrett was promoted to the board and became the fifth serving executive after Elliott, Scanlon, Lord and Nugent. Mangan and Coulstock were left to manage the breweries through 1984. 'We had friendly relationships with them,' said Elliott, 'and the business was still running well. I always had a high regard for Fred and Lou. And we did not have an obvious bloke to put in.'[26]

Of more importance was a whole strategic survey of what Elders was doing. The company already embraced more than a dozen substantial businesses, and the breweries represented a major switch in direction. 'We decided we could run four, maybe five core businesses,' said Elliott. 'In fact, our analyses at that time forged the shape that Elders has become today. We decided to concentrate on pastoral-cum-agribusiness, on brewing, on international, on finance and maybe on resources. At the same time, we decided to sell our food businesses because they could not expand internationally.'[27] This led to talks with the Goodman Fielder group about buying Elders margarine business. In the upshot, Elders acquired 21 per cent of Goodman, the seventh-largest company in New Zealand, in exchange for 13.97 per cent of Elders shares, and O. R. (Bob) Gunn joined the board.[28] Additionally, to lower the massive debt burden, non-core businesses were sold: Elders Metals, Elders Building Supplies, Elders Stores in Western Australia, the 19.6 per cent holding in the breweries' biggest can supplier, J. Gadsden, and the frozen food business General Jones. The traffic was not all one way. Elders came out of the float of Kidston Gold Mines, set to be the biggest gold miner in Australia, with a 15 per cent share and project management; it bought the Singapore merchant bank Private Investment Company for Asia (PICA), with offices in nine Asian capitals; and it acquired a 40 per cent interest in Peter Lawrence's broking house, Roach Tilley Grice & Co., which had housed Elliott a dozen years earlier, when surely he would have had no idea that in October 1984 he would manage authorised capital of $1 billion!'[29]

Politics claimed Elliott's time in a big way towards the end of 1984. After less than two years in power, Prime Minister Bob Hawke called a federal election for the first day of December, and as Liberal Party treasurer Elliott had to work the political begging bowl to finance the campaign. (He had done some campaigning of his own earlier in the year, using newspaper advertisements to promote his paper *The Need for Deregulation in Australia*.)[30] In the event, Andrew Peacock, who had followed Fraser as the party leader, did surprisingly well on the hustings, relating well with the voters, but Hawke, probably at the apogee of his popularity, won a second term for Labor.

The Elders group went into financial 1985 with consolidated fixed assets—freehold and leasehold land, buildings, plant and equipment, vehicles and so on—valued at more than $1.1 billion, nearly ninety times the valuation of Henry Jones's assets when Elliott took it over thirteen years earlier. Elliott himself had become a household name, receiving constant attention in the public prints. Jane Sullivan of the *Age* asked, 'What drives him?' and offered this answer: 'Not any particular desire for money, according to those who know him. An element of ego tripping perhaps, but also an altruistic desire to help his country and love for going into a situation and trying to fix it.'[31]

The year was to see that profile considerably enlarged. It was also to see the end of Elliott's twenty-year marriage to Lorraine. Life had become somewhat lonely for her, with Elliott flying here, there and everywhere, although he spent as many weekends as possible with her and their three children. He has described the break-up as a fact of life:

'It just didn't work out. . . . After consideration of children and things—my two eldest are grown up—you go on to the next phase of your life.'[32] But Geoff Lord has said, 'All of the team have had marriage difficulties. The major reason for John's break-up was the fact that he didn't have *time* to cope with the hassles of having a family—too much time pressure.'[33]

Lou Mangan, whose health was not robust, retired at the beginning of calendar 1985 after twelve years as chief executive of the breweries. He told Keith Dunstan, 'Our people are happy with the Elders acquisition. . . . If it hadn't been Elders it could have been somebody else. That's life in the eighties.'[34] To head up the breweries, Elliott pulled a rabbit out of the hat—or a bike rider out of Hong Kong. Peter Bartels had been running Elders' consolidated International Group, with its twenty offices around the world (three in Australasia, four in south Asia, five in north Asia, five in Europe and the Middle East, and three in the United States) from headquarters in Hong Kong. He had no experience of breweries, but beer flowed through his veins; his grandfather had the Bayview Hotel in South Melbourne and his father the Mountain View Hotel in Glen Waverley.

Lou Mangan — 'If it hadn't been Elders, it could have been somebody else.'

(It is important that as part of the Elders explosion, expansion has allowed executives to grow and thus have job satisfaction as well as considerable wealth. Several of them now run vast businesses: Bartels the breweries; Michael Nugent Elders Agribusiness, which includes Elders Pastoral; Ken Jarrett Elders Finance Group, the biggest merchant bank in Australia; Geoff Lord Elders Resources Limited, launched with Elders IXL holding 47 per cent of the issued capital; and Andrew Cummins Elders Investments Limited. Geoff Lord, who can be quite introspective for a bounding extrovert, credits Elliott with holding the team together and says, 'There is a homogeneity among us—all about the same age, all got big egoes, all want to make money and, more importantly, all want to establish a presence. Part of that can be attributed to John's influence and style. The enigma is that we are also individuals and there is competitive rivalry.'[35] John Baillieu, a whole generation older, who says he works ten times harder for Elders than he ever did as a director of CUB, has commented, 'They are an extraordinarily cohesive group, and they are extraordinarily loyal to each other—and loyal and supportive of John, and he is supportive of them. They work like hell. They are the smartest fellows I've met. I only wish I'd met them earlier—would have made more money.'[36]

Bartels's impact on the breweries was immediate. 'The first day he came in here he was sitting in there on the edge of his desk with his office *door open*,' one executive recalled.[37] 'He called the senior management in and at a round-table conference told us things that we used not to tell each other. He talked about market shares, strategy plans for the future, how much money we were going to spend on this and on that.

The Foster's Melbourne Cup —
with Elliott, Bartels and VRC
Chairman Hilton Nicholas.

Peter changed the culture very quickly, a tremendous cultural reform.'

The impact created wider repercussions. Fosters had sponsored the Caulfield Cup the year before; then on 1 April 1985 it was announced that the nation's most important horse race, an institution which brings Australia to a standstill, would be known as the Foster's Melbourne Cup! And it would carry prize money of a million dollars! (The papers carried pictures of Bartels and Hilton Nicholas, the chairman of the Victoria Racing Club, which conducts the big race at Flemington, holding the golden Melbourne Cup.) 'It was an intrusion into sacred territory and we did not know whether the public would accept it,' the general manager of the breweries' public affairs recalled. 'But at the end of the day there was no aggro.'[38] Before it could be put to the test, Bartels and Foster's intruded upon another sacred territory, the Melbourne Cricket Ground. As the massive sponsor of the Victorian Football League, Foster's mounted the half-time entertainment during the grand final in 1985 with music, a dancing display and a huge Foster's flag which sported the familiar 'F' logo and the legend 'Foster's Lager' and required more than a hundred people to carry it onto and round the oval. (A reporter for the Macquarie radio network in far-off New York started the furphy that children carried the flag and were being exploited in a crass commercial demonstration; the fact was that the carriers were all eighteen or over and had the support of their parents.)[39]

When the Foster's Melbourne Cup was run for the first time, the Prince and Princess of Wales were on hand as official guests, 1985 being Victoria's 150th birthday. The event was televised to Britain and Europe, to the United States and to Hong Kong, as well as throughout Australia, to an estimated audience of at least sixty million viewers. Prince Charles, when presenting the cup to the owners of the winner, What a Nuisance, could not have done Elliott, Bartels, *et al.* prouder; in a witty speech he said that surely the cup should have been filled with Foster's but that no doubt none was available because 'it's all being sold in England'.[40]

That was precisely what Elliott and Bartels had in mind, the complete globalisation of Foster's. To do that they needed a brewery to service Europe and another to service North America. In seeking the first, they triggered the biggest takeover battle ever in Britain and, in a bizarre twist, staged the most sensational spending spree ever seen on Australian stock exchanges.

But before those events could get under way, the year ended on sweet and sour notes. The sourness lay in two driving charges which had been hanging over Elliott for a year; he had done a U-turn while driving a friend home from the Melbourne Club lateish one night and he had been booked for (*a*) crossing double white lines and (*b*), after a test at Kew police station, for exceeding a blood-alcohol level of .05. So he appeared at Camberwell Court, where his counsel said he would plead guilty. The magistrate fined him $250 and cancelled his driving licence for six months, and fined him a further $95 for crossing the lines.[41] The sweetness came with the retirement of Sir Ian McLennan, who was nearing the end of his seventy-sixth year, as chairman of Elders IXL. Elliott has said, 'Sir Ian is, in my view, the greatest business- man that Australia has produced. Apart from anything else, he pushed BHP in oil. At Elders his leadership on both the Elders GM and CUB deals was absolutely critical.'[42] Regard was clearly mutual. For it was Sir Ian who overcame the doubts of some of the outside directors about combining the roles of chairman and chief executive. When he decided to go, he was adamant that Elliott must become Elders' executive chairman.

Next page:

Foster's Grand Final — the flag could not have been bigger.

*Prince Charles in action — he said
the Cup should have been filled with
Foster's.*

*Handing over — Sir Ian McLennan
insisted on Elliott's succession.*

chapter **7**
Globalising Foster's

Most people who are old enough remember where they were when they heard that President John F. Kennedy had been assassinated by Lee Harvey Oswald in Dallas, Texas, on 22 November 1963. All Australians who are old enough remember where they were when they heard that Edward Gough Whitlam had been sacked as Prime Minister by the man he appointed Governor General, Sir John Kerr, on 11 November 1975. And all those with the slightest interest in the money market remember where they were when they heard about the biggest buying plunge in Australian stock exchange history, on 10 April 1986. Soon after the market opened, I called into the office of a client, Information Express, a dial-up database which carried up-to-the-minute share quotes. Robert Armstrong, who had worked for years in brokers' offices, called out, 'Hey, look at this. Someone is getting stuck into BHP.' Since quotes on Information Express do not change on-screen as the market changes, he was accessing BHP over and over again to monitor transactions. They were being traded at $7.36 a share, and more than a hundred million BHP shares changed hands during that morning session. A couple of phone calls established that the brokers creating bedlam by buying were Peter Lawrence's Roach Tilley Grice, John Baillieu's E. L. & C. Baillieu and John McIntosh's McIntosh Hamson Hoare Govett. Clearly, Robert Holmes à Court, who had made several takeover attempts on BHP, was not making the on-market move. Almost as clearly, John Elliott was the architect of the raid, for the three brokers were his mates.

By the end of the morning session on the 10th, Elders had acquired about 10 per cent of BHP; by evening 15 to 16 per cent. After overnight buying in London and further buying on the 11th, Elders filed a substantial shareholding notice which disclosed that 'Elders had purchased a total of 231,028,581 shares, or 18.56 per cent, of BHP's capital'.[1]

For any event, one has to inquire: when, where, why and how? The *when* and the *where* were obvious. The *why* was of the utmost complexity.

*Elliott vs Holmes à Court —
Spooner's view in the* Age,
11 *April, 1986.*

And the *how* was a demonstration of how far the Elliott team had come
in the field of high finance and discreet operations.

Consider the *why*. It was speculated that this was round three
between Elliott and Holmes à Court. Not so; Elliott had offered to buy
the latter's BHP holding before completing his on-market raid. It was
further speculated that Elliott wished to be a white knight, defending
BHP from Holmes à Court. Again no so; his raid was a complete
surprise to the BHP directors. It was finally speculated that Elliott
was having a bit of sport at the expense of the Big Australian. In
matters concerning his shareholders, Elliott has never indulged in light
behaviour. The true explanation was much more interesting, and it
illuminated the psychologist in Elliott.

When he and Bartels determined to make Foster's a world lager, it
was obvious that a brewery in Britain, which could service continental
Europe, would have to be bought. In the northern spring of 1985 a
scouting party was established in London to survey the possibilities. It

was led by the veteran strategist Peter Scanlon—who had retired from executive duties to head up an associated company, AFP Investments (of which more later) but was still on the board—and the new company strategist Andrew Cummins, who had recently been recruited from Elliott's financial alma mater, McKinsey & Co. They were reinforced by the old hands Richard Wiesener and Bob Cowper, by then well established as merchant bankers in Monaco. The quarry they selected was Allied Lyons PLC.[2] This was a big outfit, four times the size of Elders and second only to Bass Charrington as the biggest brewer in Britain, making the old favourite Double Diamond as well as Skol lager and Long Life. It embraced the famous Lyons Corner House brasseries as well as a big chain of tearooms and was into wines and spirits and soft drinks. It employed more than seventy thousand people![3] But it was tired, and Elliott said later, 'They've got the number two beer, the number two Scotch and the number two food lines. We want to be number one in everything we do, and when we get the Allied brands we will be.'[4]

The way the team put the figures together, Elders could get Allied for perhaps £1.7 billion (about $3.4 billion at that time) and recoup say £1.2 billion by selling off the non-beer divisions and another £400 million by selling 50 per cent of each of Allied's seven thousand tied houses (hotels and public houses) to the publicans, a joint-venture plan which was working well with the CUB hotel-keepers in Australia. In other words, they could get their British brewing base for next to nothing.[5] Ever so quietly, an associate company called IXL was formed—49 per cent owned by Elders and the majority by Wiesener and Cowper, although Elders had no option to buy their 51 per cent[6]—and it started buying Allied shares. Elliott hoped to build to 10 per cent of Allied before making a public takeover bid.

In the meantime he had to raise the money. In New York he talked to Citibank, America's biggest bank, which had helped with the CUB takeover, and over a period of eight weeks he talked to six or seven other banks. He recalled: 'I went straight to the chief executives and said, "This is going to be the biggest takeover in the history of the United Kingdom. I need £2 billion." On one sheet of paper I showed them how the thing would work. And I told them, "You might have to stand up for two hundred million quid and even nine hundred million quid until we sell it down. I need to know your attitude." And they said, "In principle, yes." We built a facility for £1.8 billion for our first bid.'[7]

The risk in having to work with a consortium of banks is security. 'It was leaking out of the banks,' Elliott said; 'too much chatter.' So he was obliged to announce a bid after acquiring only 6 per cent of Allied at an average of £2.05 a share. 'We had to declare our hand or Allied could have taken defensive action. . . . Once a company is under offer in the UK it cannot issue stock or buy another company.'[8] He pitched his bid at £2.55 a share. The chairman of Allied Lyons, the dapper Sir Derrick Holden-Brown, branded it 'an impudent bid'. But *The Times*, under the headline 'Allied does not give a XXXX for Elders' (adapting the advertising that plastered London for Elliott's brewing rival Alan Bond 'An Aussie wouldn't give a XXXX for any other beer'), commented that Elliott was 'in the mould of Australian businessmen . . . who do not notice obstacles in their way'.[9] (*The Times* had every reason to know; its proprietor, Rupert Murdoch, had often ignored obstacles in London to make impudent, and usually successful, bids.)

The subsequent battle, waged largely with 'millions being spent on advertising . . . aimed at influencing barely 270 institutional fund managers who controlled more than 70 per cent of Allied's shares',[10] meant that Elders executives flew something of a shuttle service between Melbourne and London. (Flying fills a key part of the Elders culture, particularly for Elliott, Bartels and Lord. CUB says that Bartels is one of Qantas's most regular users,[11] and Lord estimates that he flies nearly a quarter of a million miles a year. 'For Hong Kong we fly through the night,' he has said, 'work the day and fly back through the night so we can work the next day.'[12] Ken Jarrett, who says, 'I don't like travelling much', averages one flight abroad every month. He recalled, 'Once last year I went to London twice in a week. Clearly that's pretty stupid.'[13] The team eat and drink a minimum while flying and sleep most of the way. So far none of them have cracked up, which is surprising.)

The City of London was generally hostile towards Elders' bid for Allied, and the Takeover Panel, a regulatory authority, asked questions about the IXL purchasing vehicle. Allied Lyons put out its formal defence document advising shareholders not to sell; then a few days later, perhaps in response to Allied's considerable lobbying power, the British government referred the whole matter to the Monopolies and Mergers Commission, effectively consigning it to limbo for months.[14]

Elliott had feared the monopoly reference for two reasons: obviously because it stalled the takeover itself and, perhaps more importantly, because the Monopolies and Mergers Commission might knock back the bid 'on the ground that Elders gearing [borrowing] ratios appeared too high'.[15] So his thoughts and actions turned to BHP: 'We started asking BHP for $1 billion to get our assets up to satisfy the UK Monopolies Commission. We saw them as the only Australian company who could afford to invest $1 billion. . . . And remember, Jim Balderstone [Sir James Balderstone, chairman of BHP] and David Zeidler [Sir David Zeidler, a director of BHP and former boss of ICI Australia] were great supporters of mine on the CBA Bank in the early days. They've always supported Elders.'[16] Elliott and Scanlon opened negotiations with BHP soon after the monopoly reference was made in London, and several suggestions were explored. While Elders had good reason to entice BHP into a relationship, the Big Australian had motivation, too; Holmes à Court, in sustained bids for BHP, had secured 0.23 per cent of its shares in 1983, 4 per cent in 1984, and by 1985 held 11 per cent and was still buying.[17] Elliott recalled 'I used to sit there at BHP and say, "This guy Holmes à Court is going to fix you right up. . . . But they kept umming and ah-ing and saying no to our proposals.'[18]

The pace quickened on 4 February 1986, when Holmes à Court announced yet another takeover bid for BHP, seeking to acquire 250 million shares and asking for a seat on the board.[19] Scanlon put a new Elders scheme to BHP (which by then had the code name Elephant—reminiscent of Tiger for Henry Jones—while Holmes à Court was Warthog!) This plan called for a BHP subsidiary in the United States to be used as a joint-venture vehicle involving BHP and Elders to buy back Holmes à Court's holding or to reduce the capital base of BHP and thus lift performance for shareholders. The BHP board agreed it should be 'developed enthusiastically', but it was eventually knocked back on legal advice.[20] A complicating factor at this stage was that Sir Roderick Carnegie wanted his CRA to buy 15 per cent of BHP's shares,[21] affording another defence against Holmes à Court. This appealed to the BHP board but not to Sir Alistair Frame, the chairman of CRA's British parent company RTZ; and at an acrimonious board meeting, in which Carnegie's considerable powers of persuasion failed, the proposal was hit on the head.[22] (Carnegie is no longer with CRA, as we shall see.)

Elders' focus was still on Allied Lyons, but time was running out; the Monopolies Commission was due to report in less than ten weeks, and the gearing sore had not been cured. So, on 26 March, two days before the Easter break, they put yet another proposal to BHP: that the Big Australian would take up one thousand redeemable preference shares in Elders for a total amount of $1 billion, 'each share comprising 10 cents capital and $999,999.90 premium, with a dividend rate of 6.75 per cent per annum on the issue price and a term of seven years. . . . Each of these 1,000 preference shares have, or will have, attached to them an option which may be exercised by taking up ordinary fully-paid $1 shares in the company at a price of $4.35 each up to a limit of 20 per cent of the issued ordinary shares.'[23] That evening, while the proposal was being discussed with BHP, Elliott was asked if he, in turn, would buy shares in BHP. He replied, 'Categorically no.'[24] The BHP board considered the proposal the next day, and Brian Loton, the chief executive, telephoned Elliott to say the directors 'considered it worth pursuing'.[25]

(Over these days the market had been startled by Elders selling all or most of the shares they had acquired in Allied Lyons for a cool profit of $83.5 million. Allied's advisers, the merchant bank of S. G. Warburg, commented, 'We very much doubt that London has seen the last of John Elliott, but we are confident that Allied has seen him off.'[26] Nothing of the kind, said Elliott. 'We believe Allied became over-priced and therefore we sold our shares.'[27] And he undertook to pursue the take-over 'with the same amount of effort'.)

Elliott spent that Easter in Tasmania. On Good Friday his mind was filled with business thoughts: 'We wanted to be friendly with BHP. But they are a slow-moving company, and the best way we could do something was to put our best foot forward.'[28] He felt the 'best foot' would be to buy a substantial parcel of BHP shares. The next morning he had a long talk on the telephone with Scanlon, who was spending Easter with his family at Sefton, the mansion (originally built by W. L. Baillieu) and Elders training centre at Macedon, to the north of Melbourne. They decided it would be a good plan tactically and psychologically for Elders to become a significant shareholder in BHP.[29]

That, then, was the *why* of the astonishing raid on BHP twelve days later. What about the *how*—the money? When Elders and BHP had discussed the joint venture using BHP's North American subsidiary to thwart Holmes à Court, Elliott and Jarrett had held preliminary discussions with Wardley Australia on funding, and they turned to them again as the lead banker. Following the Elliott-Scanlon phone conference on Easter Saturday, Jarrett was alerted to arrange an early meeting with the Wardley people.

(At the same time Andrew Cummins, who was in London on the Allied Lyons campaign, was asked to update his strategic research on BHP, whose share price had been falling, and prepare an analysis for the Elders board. His paper said the situation created 'a unique opportunity for Elders' and spelt out four scenarios: (1) Elders would buy 20 per cent of BHP, which would persuade BHP to make its $1 billion investment in Elders; (2) if BHP did not go for that investment, Elders would sell to Holmes à Court and give him control of BHP; (3) if neither BHP nor Holmes à Court played ball, Elders would hold the balance of power and be able to determine the future of BHP; (4) BHP was always a sound investment anyway, offering definite advantages to Elders shareholders.)[30]

A Wardley team of four, led by James Yonge, the managing director, flew from Sydney to Melbourne for a meeting with Elliott, Jarrett and Bruno Blosfelds of Elders' treasury. Elliott, whose appointments schedule is chronically overloaded, kept them waiting for an hour but soothed dented vanities by promising, 'We've got something to talk to you about that you'll find interesting'[31]—a loan facility of $1.87 billion! The Wardley team was very interested and soon gave approval in principle. (Three versions of a report of this meeting—the third of which varied substantially from the first two—were faxed to the Hong Kong and Shanghai Bank over Yonge's name; this aroused the curiosity of the national Companies and Securities Commission (NCSC) into the relationship existing between Elders and BHP and led to the later public inquiry or, as Keith Dunstan has described it, 'a public sideshow'.[32] The other banks to be approached were Citibank, already committed to Elders funding to take Allied Lyons, National Australia Bank and the ANZ Banking Group. Citibank declined, while the National and ANZ agreed to be in it. (An ANZ executive memoed his managing director, Will Bailey, suggesting that he 'confirm with the BHP executive that Elders acquisition is seen as friendly'.[33] Bailey did not appear to do so.)

The Citibank drop-out meant another bank had to be approached. On Monday, 7 April, Jarrett invited the Bank of Tokyo (BOT) to become involved, talking to their senior executives in Australia, Tomohiro Ishiguro and Douglas Brown. This posed a problem, 'because the concept of a takeover is virtually alien to the Japanese'.[34] The executives were obliged to make full explanations to their Tokyo headquarters, Brown faxing a handwritten note that participation would be 'both profitable and prestigious. We will be seen as helping two of Australia's largest entities and, in doing so, we will be protecting past relationships and undertakings.' It worked, and the OK arrived the next day. There remained much work to be done with the banks before the actual money would be available; Jarrett, working round the clock, thought that things would not be in place before Monday or Tuesday, 14 or 15 April. But Scanlon became worried about the secret leaking out from one of so many bankers and pressed for the raid to be mounted on Thursday, 10 April. Elliott, bold in his concepts but always cautious with financial niceties, wanted the documentation to be in place before he struck, and pressured Jarrett to make haste.[35] Then, by Wednesday, 9 April, Elliott agreed they would have to strike the following day and asked Jarrett to arrange any necessary bridging finance.

So the *how* as well as the *why* was settled. And the Elders board had approved both the raid on Elephant and the issue of the preference shares worth $1 billion earmarked for it.[36] Thus the stage was set for a riveting few hours. Flies on the walls at Garden Street (and there are not many of them) would have observed at four o'clock that Wednesday afternoon that three quite separate meetings were taking place. In the first, Elliott was planning the raid with his brokers; in the second, Jarrett was advancing the paper work with the bankers; and in the third, Scanlon was negotiating the preference-share deal with two BHP executives—and he made sure, by ushering them through a different door, that they knew nothing of the other meetings.[37]

Of his meeting with the brokers, Elliott recalled, 'I'll never forget the look of shock on a couple of faces when they realised what we were going to do'—although Baillieu as deputy chairman of Elders was in the know. 'They turned to a smile fairly quickly when they understood the implications'[38]—literally millions of dollars in broking commissions! A key issue was share price. BHP had closed that day at $6.56; Elliott was authorised by his board to go to $7.50 if necessary. The brokers said Elders would get a lot of shares at $7.40 because 'there were a lot of people who were reluctant to sell their shares to Bell [Holmes à Court]'.[39] Elliott felt that $7.30 would be enough. In the end, a compromise of $7.36 was agreed, a lift of 80 cents above current market price. The buying vehicle was to be Beswick, an Elders subsidiary incorporated in the Australian Capital Territory; the brokers were to tell sellers only that the buyer 'was not a party associated with Holmes à Court'.[40] And Elliott warned the brokers that they might be pulled out of the market at any moment because Holmes à Court might sell and there would be the risk of going beyond a safe 19.9 per cent.

The telephone start time on Thursday, 10 April, was nine o'clock, but the brokers were in their offices long beforehand, working out the institutions and investors they would call. In a special office by then, equipped with a private line which could not be traced back to Elders, was the go-between who would call Holmes à Court in Perth. This was Peter Nicholas Yunghanns, a lawyer by training but an aggressive investor and takeover man by inclination and a keen polo player. He had enjoyed a long association with the Elliott team and had indeed bought a substantial piece of Provincial Traders from them. His wealth has been estimated at $55 million[41] and $70 million.[42]

Pandemonium broke at Post Six, where BHP quotes were chalked up, the second the market opened at ten o'clock. The broking team bought and bought for thirty minutes and then were pulled out for the first time. It was time to try Holmes à Court. Elliott listened in as Younghanns made the call. It happened that Holmes à Court was at home with a head cold, and the conversation was conducted with a lieutenant who immediately sought details. He was given none but was invited to check the caller's trading bona fides with Wardley Australia, which he did.[43] The brokers were let loose again. During the lunch break, Elliott telephoned Loton at BHP and told him that Elders was a 'long-term investor'. Loton expressed surprise, which was fairly understandable.

Then, as cool as a glass of Foster's, Elliott flew away from the confusions of Melbourne to keep a promise to address the Liberal Party's dinner at Pymble Golf Club on Sydney's north shore. He stayed overnight and next day addressed the party's Sydney branch after luncheon at Menzies Hotel.[44] Meanwhile, back at BHP's 'Black Stump', BHP directors and executives were making their first real response: while Elliott was speaking at St Ives, they bought through Richard Wiesener, of all people, Elders convertible bonds for more than $200 million and, after being so dilatory for so long, began preparing an analysis of the $1 billion preference-share proposal for board consideration.[45] Elliott's hunch on Good Friday that they needed a bit of stick started to look good. Next morning, Friday, while Elliott prepared some speech notes for the Liberals, Barbara A'Beckett arranged for him and Holmes à Court to meet the next day!

Elliott returned to Melbourne that afternoon and, with Scanlon and Baillieu, met with Balderstone, Loton and two other BHP executives for some ninety minutes. Much of the chat was general, but Elliott sought a progress report on the $1 billion preference-share deal, and Loton told him that management would be recommending it to a meeting of the BHP board the following morning.[46] The stick was working even better.

Elliott and Holmes à Court met as arranged at ten o'clock on Saturday morning in Elliott's flat; they chatted for more than two hours in desultory fashion, each offering to buy the other out of their holding in BHP. Finally, as Holmes à Court testified later to the NCSC inquiry into the cross-investment between BHP and Elders IXL, giving it the best line of the whole hearing, he suggested to Elliott that a takeover of Elders might free him to pursue his interest in politics: 'We'd get control and you'd get to be Prime Minister.'[47]

The BHP board met at precisely the same time, and when it broke up Loton telephoned Elliott to report that, yes, the directors had approved the $1 billion proposal. The stick had worked. Elliott went off to the football and saw Carlton beat St Kilda by eighty-eight points.[48]

The whole exercise more than doubled shareholders' funds in the company from $688 million in 1985 to $1.86 billion in 1986. This was duly conveyed to the Monopolies and Mergers Commission in Britain, which found in Elders favour in September 1986, saying that a takeover of Allied Lyons by the company 'may not be expected to operate against the public interest'.[49] Elliott commented, 'They cleared us. The one-hundred-and-twenty-five-page monopolies report changed the City of London's whole attitude towards us; it gave us a great wrap. The attitude became: "These people are responsible managers, they know what they are doing." '[50]

Time changes circumstances, in big business as in everything else. While early in 1986 Elders were 'obsessed' with Allied Lyons,[51] by the time the commission reported, the market for Allied 'had gone too high to be safe',[52] and strategist Cummins had identified a more appealing target. Courage, the brewery that had set out to challenge CUB in Australia in the late 1960s and failed, was a different proposition in its own manor. It ranked as the fifth biggest brewery in Britain (at 3.4 million barrels of beer a year, it brewed about 65 per cent as much as the CUB breweries); it had more than 5,600 tied public houses; it owned the famous wine and spirits wholesaler Saccone and Speed, plus a chain of 386 off-licences (bottle shops).[53] Vitally, its current owners did not want it! The powerful Hanson Trust was run by a lord and a knight, Lord James Hanson in London and Sir David White in New York. They had none of the effeteness of much of the British aristocracy and were hard-nosed acquirers, rather like the Elliott team at Elders. Some six months earlier they had taken over the Imperial Group of companies, including

Courage, for £2.6 billion, or $6 billion; in the northern autumn of 1985 they wanted to sell Courage. Cummins picked up the vibes; so did Alan Bond's men at Bond Brewing, so did Alick Rankin of another substantial British brewer, Scottish and Newcastle, and so did America's biggest brewer, Anheuser-Busch, makers of Budweiser.[54]

Elders had exploratory talks with Sir David White in New York. Then, early in September—right after a three-way truce had been stitched up in Melbourne which put Elliott and Holmes à Court on the BHP board and Loton on the Elders board—Elliott and Cummins went into negotiations with Lord Hanson and his team in London. Two weeks later, crisp, clean and with none of the emotional fuss that had characterised the response to the bid for Allied Lyons, the deal was done. Elders took Courage for $3.5 billion.[55] (To take Foster's more strongly into North America, some six months later Elders also took the Carling O'Keefe breweries in Canada for $413 million.[56] Ted Kunkel, an experienced CUB executive, was sent to Toronto to take charge of this 150-year-old operation.) Much of the financing for these acquisitions was arranged by Ken Jarrett through 'the largest international multi-currency Eurobond issues ever made.'[57] Gideon Haigh, the author of *The Battle for* BHP, claims, 'Jarrett was the first Australian finance officer to realise and exploit the potential of the Euromarkets as a place for raising equity capital.'[58]

Courage and Carling gave Peter Bartels mighty launching platforms for the wider marketing of Foster's. Additionally, he retained earlier distribution arrangements reached with Watney, Mann & Truman, giv-

Elliott takes Courage — and drinks a toast with Michael Cottrell, watched by John Courage himself.

ing Foster's sales exposure in some twenty thousand pubs and restaurants in Britain.[59] He used Paul Hogan in witty advertising campaigns in both Britain and North America, and their impact was much lifted by the popularity of Hogan's *Crocodile Dundee* films. Bartels has said, 'I have seen the second and it isn't as good as the first, but there's an awful lot of Foster's in it.'[60] CUB was always big in sports sponsorships, and Bartels has vastly extended this form of promotion, not only with the Foster's Melbourne Cup and the football, but by sponsoring grand prix motor racing, which is televised internationally to huge audiences. He took over the Mitsubishi sponsorship of the Adelaide Grand Prix in 1986 and bought space for Foster's signs on the Monaco, Belgian, Austrian and Hungarian grand prix circuits, with more planned. (It was a natural for him, really, because he owns and races Porsches—including a souped-up Kremer Porsche, which carries a price tag of about $200,000—in what little spare time he has.)[61] A lieutenant has said, 'Traditionally, brewers were afraid of motor sport because of the drink-driving problem, but Peter argues, "There is no link between motor sport and driving a car. The grand prix driver is the epitome of control—a person who does not mix drinking and driving because he can't afford to; it would kill him." The grand prix exposure for Foster's with a six-hundred-million television audience world-wide lifts us into a new international league with Honda and Marlboro. We are up there with them.'[62]

Certainly the Courage takeover has worked from a marketing viewpoint. But it carried an expensive dilemma: how best to handle its more than five thousand tied pubs? The first answer was to sell to, or joint venture with, the tenants. But that didn't work (*a*) because most British innkeepers are not very entrepreneurial and (*b*) because of problems with British tax laws. The second was to float the pubs on the share market, but the crash of October 1987 wiped out that option. The third was an old Elders stratagem: 'Look to people whom we knew we could work with'.[63]

Such people were Sir Roderick Carnegie, Lloyd Williams and Ronald Walker, the original partners in the property developer Hudson Conway, which created the new Coles Myer headquarters on the former drive-in-theatre site in Toorak Road. Carnegie was, of course, Elliott's friend over many years; Lloyd Williams was a developer with a good track record who also raced horses and was part-owner of the first Foster's Melbourne Cup winner, What a Nuisance; and the lanky Ronald Walker had owned successful private businesses and was a former Lord Mayor of Melbourne. Together they owned the Melbourne Hilton Hotel near the Melbourne Cricket Ground. In fact, discussions had been going on for about a year with Elders on three fronts: the possibility of Elders taking an equity position in Hudson Conway; the development of the old CUB building at the top of Swanston Street—one of the most con-

Next page:

Foster's Adelaide Grand Prix — the way to reach a huge audience.

spicuous sites in Melbourne—into a new $300 million headquarters for Elders IXL; and a Hudson Conway participation in Courage. Carnegie, the 'significantly interested' chairman of Hudson Conway, recalled that the three propositions came together early in 1988.[64] Elliott and Walker sealed the CUB building deal over lunch at The Ritz in London. Elliott announced the creation of the Courage Pub Company in London in May ('he smoked seven cigarettes during the 40-minute press conference').[65] Matthew Stevens reported for readers of *Business Review Weekly*: 'The deal is exceptionally good for Hudson Conway. The Australian property-development group gets 50 per cent of one of the biggest pub estates in Britain for an actual outlay of £20 million ($50 million). Elders will put in, through a preference share issue, £130 million, which will be used to finance the rest of Hudson Conway's entry cost of £150 million. Elders also will contribute £150 million for its share of the Courage Pub Company.'[66] The rest of the money for the $3 billion deal came from two established banking friends, Citibank and Credit Suisse First Boston.[67] It was a good deal for Elders, too. First, its subsidiary Elders Investments Limited (Chief Executive Andrew Cummins, who supervised the truly massive paper work in the Pubco creation) owns 30 per cent of Hudson Conway. Secondly and more importantly, because of the way it was managed, 'Elders balance sheet [would] show the company [was] virtually debt free at balance date.'[68] And thirdly and most importantly, Elders would reap the rent increases on the pubs. 'We've set a fixed rental to Hudson Conway for ten years,' Elliott said. 'But we have a head lease over all the pubs so that improved rentals over those years all come to Elders. They will share fifty per cent of capital gains, but all the income gains come to us. It's a great growth opportunity.'[69]

Bartels's distribution through Courage and the Watney chain is excellent in middle and southern England and particularly strong in and around London, but it is poor in the north and woeful in Scotland. To combat that, money has been invested in Edinburgh-based Scottish and Newcastle, the sixth biggest brewer in Britain with more than a thousand tied houses; the purchase of Sir Ron Brierley's 6 per cent stake in June 1988 took Elders to 8.92 per cent of Scottish. Elders called it a 'strategic investment', but Scottish's Alick Rankin found it 'unwelcome, unless it is long-term and supportive'.[70] It possibly was, because the full takeover of another British brewery would probably put Elders back before the Monopolies and Mergers Commission. What Elders was likely doing was bringing pressure to bear on Scottish to distribute Foster's up north, a thing it had previously refused to do.[71] The bigger battle will be waged in Europe from the early 1990s, when all national trade barriers come down, creating a single marketplace with some 323 million consumers—and/or drinkers—nearly 70 per cent greater than the United States.[72] For this huge opportunity, several reports had Elders

The Pubco deal — Bartels, Elliott, Lloyd Williams and Ronald Walker.

looking for brewery sites in southern Europe or eyeing the takeover chances for such famous beers as Heineken, Löwenbräu or Carlsberg. As it is, the three Courage breweries, on which the company has been spending millions to update them, provide useful launching pads for Foster's invasion of Europe.

For the time being, Bartels and his boys have been doing just fine. In the first two months of 1988, Foster's sales in Britain went up by 10 per cent—compared with Alan Bond's XXXX increase of 1 per cent—to take the third-biggest-selling lager spot from Carlsberg;[73] and Foster's, with 6 per cent of the lager market, showed a clean pair of heels to the world's biggest-selling beer, Budweiser, which, after four years of trying, had barely 1 per cent.[74] Praise came from Norman Strauss, a London marketing consultant who advises British brewers: 'Foster's got into the British lager-drinking culture with the humour of its advertisements and an unerring eye for the pub lifestyle.'[75] In recognition of this, perhaps, the Australian Marketing Institute gave the 1988 Sir Charles McGrath Award for Marketing Excellence to Peter Bartels.

(Even for the best there are pitfalls. In mid-1988, Elders IXL Wine and Spirits, a subsidiary that comes under Bartels, was set to launch a new range of spirit-based drinks called Kix with a $2 million advertising campaign when some retailers and medical people complained that they were aimed at teenagers. The *Australian Financial Review* headlined, 'Elders' Kix hit for six as Liquorland says we'll have nix.'[76] The *Australian* ran a tut-tutting editorial but concluded, 'Fortunately, Elders-IXL has recognised the damage that could have resulted from the Kix campaign. The company has withdrawn the advertisements, and in effect the product, and by doing so has shown a welcome acknowledgement of its responsibility to young Australians.'[77])

Elders Brewing Group is the company's biggest manufacturer and marketer and the biggest generator of profit (35 per cent of total profits in 1987).[78] But it is by no means the whole story of the Elders explosion.

chapter 8
The Empire Strikes Outwards

Five years after the latest new dimension was given to Elders through the acquisition of CUB in 1983, Elliott was able to say, 'We are building a major international corporation now. We are as well known in London as we are in Australia. I don't think there is any doubt that we will become the biggest Australian company, bigger than BHP. We have more natural growth.'[1]

But there had been recent frustrations. The world-wide sharemarket crash of October 1987 reduced Elders share price from a year's high of $6.12 to a woeful low of $2.70, and nine months later it was still trading in the $3.20s,[2] making the shares a steal—although that last price has to be adjusted for a one-for-four bonus issue. While the crash affected the company's activities hardly at all, it meant that a major reconstruction had to be put on hold, but by no means abandoned. It had been planned, and announced, to float Elders Brewing, Elders Finance and Elders Agribusiness to join Elders Resources and Elders Investments (unluckily listed in Hong Kong at the very time of the crash) as subsidiary public companies. Elders IXL was to retain a majority of the shares, with 35 per cent being put on offer, existing shareholders having entitlements. As the annual report said, 'This will enable sharemarkets to place a more realistic value on each of the businesses.'[3]

Such a plan was possible only because the company was effectively structured already into five core businesses or groups, created in the mid-1980s and each being built up for all they were worth by their highly competitive chief executives. We have seen already a good deal of Peter Bartels's Brewing Group; we turn now to the others.

Ken Jarrett's Elders Finance Group
Elders Finance Group became a separate entity four or five years ago when Elders Finance, Lensworth Finance and rural lending operations were drawn together and 'we started managing it as a finance house instead of as a whole lot of investments in finance subsidiaries'.[4] It is

now the biggest merchant bank in Australia with assets of more than $4 billion, and it has funds under management of more than $2 billion.[5] In financial 1987 it made a net profit of $62.5 million, a lift of 83 per cent over financial 1986, and contributed 15 per cent of Elders IXL's total profit.[6] That year, too, the thrust was expanded. In response to clients' demand for global financial services, activities were reorganised from an Australian operation with world-wide branches to an international one with a complete management structure in each region: Australia (John D. Crosby in charge), New Zealand (Max Ware), Asia (Brian K. Wagar), UK–Europe (George Ziller) and North America (Ravi Ravindran). Each region has specialists in such market disciplines as bullion, options, foreign exchange, swaps, investment management and trade finance, and all are in touch by means of an on-line global communications system. The group has a staff of more than fifteen hundred. (In 1987 again, the Elders investment in stockbrokers Roach Tilley Grice & Co was lifted to 70 per cent, although the firm remained independently managed by Peter Lawrence and his chairman Ian Roach.[7] And in 1988 they bought a New Zealand broking firm, Francis Allison Symes Ltd, of Wellington.)

Ken Jarrett — finance round the world.

During 1988, Jarrett and his team made a play for Sir Ron Brierley's 38 per cent stake in the New Zealand insurance and finance house NZI Corporation, but according to Brierley's people, as reported in *Business Review Weekly*, they 'made something of a farce of the tendering process first by contacting other potential tenderers about their intentions and second by leaking the results' of their own inquiry which 'uncovered huge potential losses in the NZI loan book'.[8] The eventual buyer was Britain's third-biggest general insurance group, General Accident, and Brierley's profit of $68 million was much lower than he had expected.[9]

Another New Zealand target that at the time of writing was bound to stir Jarrett into diligent action was the Bank of New Zealand, which was advertised for privatisation sale in Treasurer Roger Douglas's budget speech in July.[10] Elders had tried hard years earlier to win a banking licence in Australia but were knocked back by Paul Keating. New Zealand presented a back-door option.

Down the track, Jarrett sees insurance as a necessary third arm to the business. 'One way or another we'll get a commercial banking arm,' he has said. 'We have an investment banking arm which does deals, and we need to get into one more business. That's insurance.'[11]

Michael Nugent's Elders Agribusiness Group

Elders Agribusiness Group is the popular face of Elders, the red, white and blue signs of 'Elders Pastoral' atop some 450 branches in country towns of any size throughout Australia and New Zealand. Here is adventure, for the other side of the group is pushing further and further into the hazardous world of commodity trading—wool, meat, brewing

Michael Nugent — agribusiness round the world.

materials and grain, especially grain—where risk management is a 24-hours-a-day responsibility and the bottom line is an average margin of just 1.25 per cent![12]

Agribusiness has two arms: farm services through Elders Pastoral and agricultural processing and trading. In the mid-1980s, farm services were the big sales generator, accounting for 55 per cent of Elders' total sales in 1984.[13] They handled half the wool going through the Australian auction system. But they stumbled. The absorption of the acquired AML & F branches was handled badly; they 'closed the AML & F branch and fired the guys and then tried to keep the business'.[14] Their very bigness was a problem; the man on the land demands personal relationships, not anonymity. And this was heightened by the massive promotions for Foster's. As Michael Hamilton of Elders Pastoral said, 'A large part of our clientele were saying, "Elders, as we understood it, is now a brewery." And our competitors were saying every week, "Elders is going to sell its pastoral business." Indeed, John [Elliott] was furious: "How many more times do I have to say it is not for sale?" We had problems.'[15] A pessimistic estimate was that they lost one client in four,[16] which is not easy to do in the country where people are slow to change, and their share of the wool brokerage dropped to about 40 per cent.[17] But new services, including such things as a Videotext database carrying latest prices to branches and clients, better advice from agricultural chemicals, plus the fundamental requirement of providing top person-to-person service from the branches, has turned the tide.[18] Their market share in wool handling has held over the last eighteen months.[19] And excellent prices, particularly for wool, have lifted spirits throughout rural Australia.

Agricultural processing and trading faced no such problems, largely because the group was breaking new ground. Elders is now the biggest buyer of wool through the auction system to trade it on; it actively supports the market price and, at the height of the wool boom in 1988, was holding more bought bales in store than the Australian Wool Corporation held in its national stockpile.[20] Elders were adding value to wool, too, through their scouring and carbonising plants in Australia and a top-making mill in Europe.[21] In meat, they were feed-lotting on three properties, producing high-quality cuts for Japan and the top end of the Australian market and manufacturing beef for the United States. The company puts two hundred thousand grain-fed cattle through its feed lots a year, and Nugent forecasts big increases: 'I reckon the Japanese market will double in the next three or four years. Korea is opening up again and meat consumption is going up throughout Asia.' He added sagely, 'The Japanese are buying meatworks in Australia.'[22] The brewing-materials division sold nearly half a million tonnes of malt world-wide in 1987, but somewhat surprisingly sold its own creation of some fifteen years earlier, Australian Hop Marketers, and all its hop

Beef city — top meat for Japan.

gardens in Tasmania, Victoria and Britain to the world's largest hop grower, American-based John I. Hass, in 1988.[23]

The group's greatest growth excitement was vested in the fiercely competitive grain trade. From a domestic base in Australia, Elders spent the years 1983–87 going international, including buying grain elevators in four American states—Kansas, Texas, Nebraska and Iowa (bought a meat works in Iowa, too)—and the Canadian prairie province of Manitoba. As a result, by 1988 the grains division had as many assets as all of Elders Pastoral.[24] Losses on grain in financial 1986 were turned into profits in financial 1987, and in 1988 it was the grains division which pushed the Agribusiness profit up 250 per cent to some $100 million before tax, second only to the brewing profits.[25] It gave Michael Nugent great satisfaction to see that his team of international grain traders, led by Michael Furzer, were pushing up into the biggest league—the five family-owned firms of Continental (the Fribourgs), Bunge (the Hirsches and the Borns), Cargill (the Cargills and the MacMillans) and the Louis-Dreyfuses and the Andrés which have ordered how the world gets its daily bread for generations, frontiers and wars notwithstanding.[26] With a turnover of $8 billion in financial 1988, Nugent is confident that he has passed the big non-family trader Con-Agra of America ($4 to $5 billion) and is catching up on Louis-Dreyfus of France and Continental (about $12 billion), but has a fair step to go to reach Cargill's turnover in the order of $20 billion—but he is determined to try.[27]

Geoff Lord — resources round the world.

Geoff Lord's Elders Resources

Any connection between the *modus operandi* of Elders Resources and that of Henry Jones when Elliott was developing it is strictly intentional. Management takeovers are what Geoff Lord is into; he calls it 'the Elders style'. And it has worked for him. 'This company started two-and-a-half years ago with nothing [$100 million],' he said in 1988. 'It is now a $2 billion enterprise.'[28]

The company was created in 1985 by selling Elders' 19.6 per cent holding in Bridge Oil and its 15 per cent holding in Kidston Gold Mines and its 100-per-cent-owned mining division—which embraced construction, extraction and development—into Mungana Mines Limited, a gold explorer and miner, in return for large share placements and issues. Elders finished with 47.5 per cent of the reshaped company, which changed its name to Elders Resources, with Elliott as chairman and Lord managing director. As with all Elders companies, Elders Resources was carefully structured into divisions—investment, development, operations, resource finance and joint venturing, marketing and North America—and decision-making was pushed down, giving divisional heads the chance to perform for the shareholders. (Michael Hamilton, actually of Elders Pastoral, has put the philosophy very clearly: 'We all know that we work in a performance-oriented environment. If we don't perform, we go.'[29])

In its first year, Elders Resources brought its wholly owned Red Dome gold mine into production; it now pours seventy thousand ounces of gold a year. Lord, probably the most go-getting of all Elliott's recruits (who says, 'Ego is the biggest driving force in the Elders team'[30]) sought and found investment opportunities. Along the way, for example, he bought the Kaiser Engineers Group in America (which originally made its name during World War II by building Liberty Ships in three days!) for a reported $75 million and next day sold all its operations except its Australian subsidiary to the American Capital and Research Group. This meant that he acquired the successful Kaiser Engineers (Australia), which first worked on the Snowy Mountains hydro-electric scheme and has built a number of major mining facilities, for virtually nothing.[31]

(A particularly interesting investment is the 22 per cent holding in the recently merged North Broken Hill–Peko-Wallsend mining operation.[32] It brings back memories and offers much for the future. When the team was realising the assets of Henry Jones back in the 1970s, Bob Cowper, as the investment whizz, secretly assembled a 7.5 per cent parcel in NBH by buying night after night in London in the names of nominees. Then the CBA bank, which was anxious about *its* investment in the Elliott team, insisted that the parcel be sold. Tim Clark, chairman of the company and the bank's representative, sold it one night in the Melbourne Club to Consolidated Goldfields.[33] Today the company is back

Red Dome — pouring the first gold.

into NBH and Elliott and Lord joined its board in August 1988, prompting the Melbourne *Herald* financial columnist Terry McCrann to write, under the headline 'Elliott opening the back door for North BH', 'Without wishing to denigrate any of the existing North directors, as soon as Mr Elliott walks into his first board meeting, the company is his—by sheer force of personality and entrepreneurial drive. Plus the single biggest shareholding.'[34]

Andrew Cummins — strategy round the world.

Lord, always seeking to expand his company, started looking for a merger partner shortly before the market crash of October 1987. He found out that New Zealand Forest Products, with $3.3 billion in assets and $2.5 billion turnover, which five years before was New Zealand's biggest company, was in trouble. 'It was dead,' he said, 'just like Henry Jones and Elders GM were when we moved in.'[35] He started investigating, and his office explained his absences across the Tasman as fishing trips; John Durie, then the 'Bourse Sauce' columnist of the *Australian Financial Review*, dubbed him the 'trout fisherman', and the name has stuck. Early in 1988, Lord and Elliott organised a reverse takeover of NZFP in the mould of the earlier Elders GM and CUB deals, moving in management and changing the name to Elders Resources NZFP, which one can safely assume will become simply Elders Resources again in good time. Lord immediately announced sales of unsuitable assets worth $800 million, saying, 'Our first priority is to get cash flow.'[36]

Elders Investments Limited
Elders Investments Limited was established in 1987 to focus upon international investment opportunities. Incorporated in Bermuda, it was floated in Hong Kong at the unluckiest possible time, just when the stock exchange there closed down for a week following the October crash. Its share price was hit and it reported a loss to 31 December of some $20 million 'attributed to write-downs post-crash'.[37] But it has some good base investments, including pieces of Hudson Conway and Sundor, a fast-growing fruit-juice company in the United States. Like Englishmen, it just needs time.

All this splintering into groups and separate companies might suggest that Elliott, in giving his lieutenants the chance to do their own thing, has worked himself out of a job. But he remains the chairman of them all as well as chairman and chief executive of the parent company. He and Andrew Cummins also remain the top strategy consultants for all the operations. Peter Scanlon says, 'John's role today is to talk to people. To bankers—we would not have done the deals we have without John's charismatic, up-front ability to convince people of his credibility, of his capacity to borrow big sums of money and pay them back. But not only bankers; he talks to brokers, to the institutions, to politicians. That's what his life is all about, that's his job—at which he is absolutely fantastic.'[38]

chapter 9
Politics, Business, Football

More and more Elliott talks to politicians or, at any rate, talks politics. The talk-load became much heavier when he became federal president of the Liberal Party in February 1988. Only the year before, friends in the 500 Club had tried very hard to arrange for him to be the Liberal candidate in John Gorton's old seat of Higgins, held for a dozen years by Roger Shipton, but they did not manage it and he was spared a full parliament in opposition. The job of president has meant a speaking engagement almost every night that he has spent in Australia; indeed, he would have had to speak about five times every night if he had accepted all invitations from party branches and organisations.[1] It has meant sustained television and radio exposure. And it has meant, too, that Labor leaders have increased markedly their attacks on him, for they recognise him as a political opponent who poses great danger to their retaining power. Finance Minister Peter Walsh, using the protection of parliamentary privilege, accused Elliott of defrauding shareholders; he has not been prepared to repeat it under circumstances which would allow the victim to sue for slander.[2] Treasurer Paul Keating, who so badly wants to be prime minister, reacted to an Elliott critique of Australia's recent economic record in this fashion: 'If Mr Elliott could rise above his sectional, partisan pettiness and start thinking in national terms about the kind of modern complexion the Australian economy now has, including its tax and competitive structure, then he might say something which helps Australia rather than hinders it.'[3] Prime Minister Hawke, pricked by an Elliott criticism of Keating's economic statement in May 1988, invited him in full television close-up to 'whack off'.[4] (*Concise Oxford Dictionary*: 'whack . . . strike heavily with stick'—surely not the word the prime minister really had in mind.)

Liberals who crowded to hear Elliott at gatherings all round the nation were treated to an exposition of his three public passions: politics, business and football. Sometimes he juggled the order—football,

Robust rejoicing — Elliott with Wayne 'The Dominator' Johnston, Carlton's best player in the 1988 Qualifying Final of the VFL; three broken ribs the following week put him out of the series (courtesy of the Sun News Pictorial).

business and politics—because those three strands have been spun into a thread which represents his approach to action. When introduced to the Young Presidents' Organisation, top entrepreneurs and business people from all over the world who came to Australia in January 1988 for the Bicentenary, he was described as a leading businessman and a conservative political leader, but he started on another tack: 'My greatest claim to fame is to be president of the Carlton Football Club, the best club in the Victorian Football League; it's won more premierships than any other club, has more supporters, has more money.' Then he asked the rhetorical question: 'What things make Carlton such a good club?', and answered, 'Strong leadership, singularity of purpose—to win—guided democracy, and the pursuit of excellence. . . . What you need are good players, a good coach, good strategy and a lot of determination and team spirit.' He said the same characteristics are required for success in business and, indeed, in national life 'to make Australia great again'.[5] Elliott told his international audience that Australia, over the two hundred years of largely white development, had enjoyed periods of greatness. Why?

The people who came here in the early days had a singular purpose: to make a go of it, to forge a new life, to turn adversity to advantage. Mateship developed out of trying circumstances, and within such a small nation there was an enormous determination to succeed. There were no class barriers, and there was virtually no bureaucracy. . . . The first great period of growth came with the rush of immigration to the goldfields in the 1850s. And by 1900 Australia was the richest country in the world for its population. . . . But then the first significant decline set in: federalism, income tax brought in as a temporary measure, and the establishment of Canberra as the national capital, right outside the main stream of Australian life. . . . The second great period of growth came after World War II with another mighty wave of immigration. Again why? Strong leadership. Go back to football, go back to business. Menzies became prime minister, Tom Playford ran South Australia, and Henry Bolte became premier of Victoria—all strong men. The purpose at that time was to make Australia a much better place, to grow. We had twenty dynamic years—by 1970 we were still in the top six countries of the world by GNP. . . . Then the malaise set in.

The malaise started when Menzies retired and Harold Holt drowned. The Liberal Party lost its leadership, although it remained in government.

Then came Gough Whitlam—the woefulness of the Whitlam Labor years. He presumed that economic prosperity would continue and set out to create a society that did more for people; but economies worldwide were turning down, and there was a doubly bad reaction. And the public service became politicised for the first time in Australia.

Then we had the unfulfilled promise of Malcolm Fraser; the rhetoric was right but the performance was not. And now we have the cynicism of Hawke.

What has happened through the 1970s and 1980s is that the cohesion disappeared. Whitlam's actions and Fraser's actions over supply divided Australian society. The leadership was gone, the teamwork disappeared, the mentality of society changed; Australians began to say, 'We are owed a living; everyone deserves a bigger slice of the cake.'

Look at the decline over the last twenty years: the highest deficits, the highest interest rates, huge balance-of-payments problems, massive debt problems, big increases in taxation, new taxes, wages not geared to productivity, and, in a sense, the trade unions have been able to act above the law.

We've got a malaise in our value systems. It is now being said that governments solve things better than individuals—free education, free health care, dole without work, and every special-interest group gets looked after if it yells loud enough—at the expense of the silent majority. It was a Liberal government which decided to create this multiracial thing when, in fact, our immigrants in the past helped to create a homogeneous Australia—the Silvagnis and the Jesaulenkos [Carlton footballers Sergio Silvagni and Alex Jesaulenko] saw themselves as Australians first, not Italians or Yugoslavs.

(Quite often Elliott detours to talk about his grandmother: 'My grandmother, who died at ninety-six, would not accept a pension because the stigma of welfare was so bad to her. "Only the poor people did that," she would say. But today welfare is looked upon as a benefit and no longer a stigma.' He laments, too, the loss of patriotism—'the knocker syndrome, trying to bring down the successful, slashing the tall poppies.')

By the nature of the man, the dirge is only an introduction; the negatives set up the positives. He says simply, '*We have to reset our value systems.*' How? 'You go back to philosophy first. From your philosophy you can establish policies and then you can determine actions—exactly as you do in business.'[6]

The fountainhead of Liberal philosophy, strongly called upon by Elliott, was Robert Gordon Menzies and the things he wrote and said when he brought the scattered conservative forces together in the spring of 1944 to launch the radical Liberal Party of Australia. 'We took the name Liberal,' Menzies wrote in his memoirs, 'because we were determined to be a progressive party, willing to make experiments, in no sense reactionary but believing in the individual, his rights, and his enterprise, and rejecting the Socialist panacea.'[7] At his inaugural conference of fourteen factions in Canberra, Menzies spoke of the need to encourage thrift and saving, investment and reward: 'The principle of such reward, sometimes sneered at as exhibiting the profit motive, is the dynamic force of social progress and is of the essence of what we call private or individual enterprise.' Menzies made the point that 'governments do not provide enterprise; they provide controls' and went on: 'There cannot be rising living standards if all we propose to do is to redistribute what we now have. We must produce more and produce it more cheaply if we are to survive and grow.' And he concluded: 'I see the individual and his encouragement and recognition as the prime motive force for the building of a better world. Socialism means high costs, inefficiency, the constant intrusion of political considerations, the damping down of enterprise, the overlordship of routine. None of these elements can produce progress, and without progress security will turn out to be a delusion.'[8]

Menzies did unite the conservatives, and the whole thing was put to the test in the election campaign of 1949. He declared what he called 'the heart of Liberalism' in his policy speech: 'The real freedoms are to worship, to think, to speak, to choose, to be ambitious, to be independent, to be industrious, to acquire skill, to seek reward. These are the real freedoms, for these are the essence of the nature of man.'[9] The electors agreed with him—and he was prime minister for a record seventeen years straight.

Elliott believes that Liberal philosophy has changed very little since Menzies drafted the platform of the party more than forty years ago. In his speeches he takes sections of the platform and shows how philosophy translates into policies:

> If you believe that everyone who wants a job deserves one, and that we want to raise the standard of living of our citizens, we have got to get Australia competitive, got to foster economic growth and got to start populating the country.
>
> If we are going to reward entrepreneurial spirit and hard work, we have to have a tax system which provides incentives to do that. We have to reduce regulation and speed decision-making in the bureaucracy. We have to take the rigidities out of the system, particularly in the labour market, and we've got to eliminate the hand-out mentality. We must become pleased that wealth is being generated in our society.
>
> If we accept that individuals *can* do it better than government (basically I believe we do all believe that, although actions over time have shown that we think governments must do it better because we let them!), then we must reduce the size of the bureaucracy, reduce government spending, reduce regulation and privatise those government institutions which would be run better by individuals.
>
> If we are going to increase individual freedoms, we must reduce dependence on government and reduce what I call collectivism—that is, the power of the trade unions and, in my view, things like the Business Council; the Business Council is simply a device to stop businesses talking to government. We must also revise the wage-fixing system.
>
> If we want to reinforce the importance of the family, we must give preferences in taxation to housing. (That is one of my very few socialist views; I think home ownership is so important—we have the highest level in the world—and it makes everybody a mini-capitalist because they have an asset!)
>
> If we are going to look after the poor and the unfortunate—which we must—we need a welfare system based on need, not one stretching right through the middle class. Better to have lower taxes so they can look after themselves; we should only directly look after the people who cannot look after themselves.[10]

Elliott likes to wind up his speeches by citing the tenets of the great American president, Abraham Lincoln (and was tickled to hear them quoted by Margaret Thatcher, his political heroine, when she visited

Mark Knight, Melbourne Herald, March, 1988.

Australia in the winter of 1988): (1) you cannot bring about prosperity by discouraging thrift; (2) you cannot strengthen the weak by weakening the strong; (3) you cannot help the wage earner by pulling down the wage payer; (4) you cannot keep out of trouble by spending more than you earn; (5) you cannot build character and courage by taking away man's incentive and independence; (6) you cannot help men permanently by doing for them what they could and should be doing for themselves.[11]

(These principles are reflected in Elders IXL benefactions to worthy causes, which are made quietly but amount to some $1.5 million a year. 'We help those who help themselves,' Elliott has said. 'We don't, for example, give to hospitals which are government sponsored.'[12] An approach from the Howard Florey Institute of Experimental Physiology and Medicine at the University of Melbourne concerning a genetic engineering probe into the expression of particular cloned genes led Elliott into committing Elders to provide $100,000 a year for five years.[13] For a long time, in the depressed areas of Tasmania which were associated with the original Henry Jones, Elders have provided scholarships for children. And for the bicentennial year, Elders put $1 million into the restoration of the old Henry Jones sailing vessel *Alma Doepel*, 151 tonnes gross,[14] which became one of the Tall Ships fleet and is now a training ship for youngsters.)

Elliott's political beliefs are often tested on radio. He became something of a regular on Michael Schildberger's program on the ABC's 3LO, often creating a furore. One, early in 1988, concerned indirect taxation. Just back from overseas, he told listeners that many efficient nations

Restoring the Alma Doepel — 'We help those who help themselves.'

levied a consumption tax on purchases and were thus able to lower income tax. 'We should have a consumption tax in Australia,' he said. This was not stated Liberal policy and the media had a lovely time beating up the question: Who makes policy, the leader (John Howard) and his MPs or the president? A couple of months later, on the same program, he attacked the government's abolition of investment allowances on new plant and equipment and revealed, 'We are surveying to see if we should be producing Foster's elsewhere. It's a great worry—that the tax system creates that sort of situation.'[15] It was newspaper reports of this statement which led Hawke to tell Elliott to 'whack off'. Called by the ABC's 'AM' program next morning, Elliott said that was 'a very petulant remark'.[16] Also with Schildberger, he was questioned about the proposed treaty with Aborigines and echoed John Howard: 'We don't want a treaty which creates two classes of citizen.' And about land rights: 'Every time a mineral discovery is made in this country, some Aboriginal group claim it as an important sanctuary or burial ground or something or other. The Australian people are getting sick of it.' Again with Schildberger, he declared, 'This multiculturalism is a load of nonsense.[17]

All this seemed miles away from the Elders boardroom, and there was no doubt that Liberals at branch level and party supporters—probably a strong majority—hoped profoundly that Elliott would throw his hat into the political ring; they perceived him as a winner and John Howard and Andrew Peacock as losers. As more Liberals met and talked with him, there was the realisation, too, that he has a charming directness which is not part of his image as a corporate tycoon or a Carlton fan who is prepared to put his money where his mouth is in

$10,000 wagers on the result of a match.[18] While it is widely known that Margaret Thatcher uses great feminine charm as well as political acumen to get her way, it is not too fanciful to hazard the guess that Elliott's openness and geniality would be political advantages.

A crucial question for Elders is: What would happen if Elliott did decide to move? When Trevor Kennedy asked him about that in 1987, he replied, 'I've got succession well planned at Elders. . . . The business has to be able to go on whether I'm here or not. Part of the restructuring of Elders has made it easier to handle the succession problems.'[19]

In his personal life, Elliott followed new directions in 1987. He became a client of Elders Pastoral by buying two rural properties, and, of much more moment, he married again. The property where he weekends when possible is Wooroma, 9,440 hectares of top Merino sheep country near Moulamein in the Riverina. It has water licences, and he is extending irrigation to some six hundred hectares. Although the historic homestead was burned down ten years ago, it has been faithfully recreated. When Graeme Beck, manager of Elders Pastoral at Deniliquin, drove him out to inspect the place, Elliott said, 'You've told

Mark Knight, Australian Financial Review 8 *April*, 1987.

me how good it is. Now tell me what's wrong with it.' Beck replied, 'It's a fair way from an airport. And it's got a manual telephone.'[20] Undaunted by such isolation, Elliott bought it for $110 an acre ($272 a hectare)—and has seen the market value double since.[21] The second is in Victoria, with the rivers Murray and Goulburn forming two of the boundaries.

His new wife is the former Amanda Drummond-Moray, of the country family Bayles of Nagambie in central Victoria; her father, Ian N. Bayles, DFC, is a committeeman of the VRC, a grazier and a company director. Elliott introduced his elegant consort to friends during the football season. He bought a penthouse in Barridene, 'one of the best apartment buildings' in Toorak Road,[22] as their Melbourne base and a vast villa, Cuccia Noye, at Saint-Jean-Cap-Ferrat, in the South of France, as their European headquarters.[23] Indeed, all good things came together for Elliott that September: Elders announced record net profits of over $400 million for the year, up more than 100 per cent on the previous year;[24] Carlton won the VFL grand final for the first time in his presidency; and he was married at St Johns, Toorak, and then taken by helicopter to the splendid reception afterwards at Sefton.

John and Amanda Elliott.

Rondo:

To the Victor Belong the Spoils

If an investor had put a thousand dollars into the Elliott team the day they walked into Henry Jones IXL in 1972 and had reinvested the dividends year by year and held onto all the bonus issues, what would that investment be worth in Elders IXL shares in 1988?[1] Charles Faggotter, the company secretary and one of the longest-surviving Elders GM men from Burra in South Australia, knows the answer upon the instant: $74,650. Put another way, if the invester had put in fourteen thousand dollars—the price of a reasonable second-hand car these days—he or she would be worth a million and more. That is the measure of what the team has done for their shareholders. It is an impressive performance over just sixteen years.

What have the team got to show for their labours? Richard Wiesener and Bob Cowper, who called it quits after the first ten years, left with enough money to launch themselves as merchant bankers in Monaco and are very comfortable; Richard Wiesener, according to both *Business Review Weekly* and *Australian Business*, is worth $80 million and Bob Cowper is worth anything between $20 million (AB) and $100 (BRW).[2] Peter Scanlon, who went off to become something of a business doctor but remains on the Elders board, was worth $120 million according to BRW before the crash of October 1987 and $30 million according to AB post-crash. Again, very comfortable.

The team still in harness receive 'first, adequate, but not big, salaries; secondly, bonuses directly related to performance, and thirdly, shares—the company share scheme, involving many thousands of staff, is a very good incentive.'[3] For the top seven executives there is now in place an ownership position in a company called Harlin—more of that in a moment. The seven are John Elliott, Geoff Lord, Peter Bartels, Ken Jarrett, Michael Nugent, Andrew Cummins and Ken Biggins, the boss of administration and services for Elders IXL.[4]

A company called AFP was mentioned earlier. This was originally Australian Farming Property, a 'none-too-promising rural company' of which Elliott and John McIntosh, the stockbroker and Carlton fan, bought 42 per cent five years ago.[5] When Peter Scanlon wanted to do his own thing, he moved into this unlikely vehicle and it became AFP

Investments, one of the dashing performers of the 1980s share boom. Elliott sold his interest, but McIntosh hung in.[6] In a rather complicated way, the details of which are too tedious to canvass here, Scanlon and AFP became the negotiating custodians of the Elders executives' financial destiny. By mid-1988 that destiny rode with Harlin, the potential owner of 31.75 per cent of the shares of Elders IXL. Elliott explained: 'Harlin bought BHP's holding in Elders, about eighteen per cent, and it bought the share options that AFP held in Elders. If all those options were to be converted, Harlin would have just on 32 per cent of Elders. The executives have had to subscribe real money for their equity base in Harlin; they have about 30 per cent of that company. The Elders Super Fund is the biggest shareholder with about 35 per cent, AFP has about 20 per cent, and the balance are held by outside people.'[7]

It was through the long relationships with Citibank and Wardley—and, indeed, BHP—that the necessary financing could be arranged. 'How else would a working-class guy like me get a slice of such a leveraged position?' asks Geoff Lord. The fact is that the seven will have to find some $1.7 billion in 1993 or, at any rate, be in a position to refinance it. Lord again: 'Obviously if the Elders share price has gone up, or the earnings have gone up or whatever, we can make some money out of the equities. The price we're paying to get in is higher than the market, and there are no dividends coming to us for five years. So there's no free ride. The advantage is in the volume and the leverage; but it's only an advantage if it works.'[8]

The Harlin arrangement aroused some chatter, perhaps motivated by envy. A waspish cover story in *Business Review Weekly*, headlined 'Big Bad John', reported that some institutional investors, particularly overseas, had backed off Elders, but it noted that powerful National Mutual, a backer from the beginning, remained 'the biggest share buyer' in Elders.[9] (The relationship between National Mutual and the team has never wavered; today Elliott sits on the National Mutual board and National Mutual's chairman, Bails Myer, is one of the longest-serving Elders directors.) John Baillieu, the patriarch of the Elders board who wears his own wealth with the comfort of a second skin, perhaps has the right perspective: 'They thoroughly deserve to make the money. Elliott has always looked after the shareholders. The team has total identity with the shareholders because of their own shareholding interest.'[10]

It is this personal involvement which motivates the team to globalise not only Foster's but every facet of the huge company's operations. They are even taking to the United States the branch concept of Elders Pastoral, the very business that Thomas Elder started building so long ago. It is with pride that Elliott says, 'Elders is the second-highest profit earner in the country, second only to BHP. Elders has outstripped Coles

Myer as the number one in sales revenue, and, with News Corporation, Elders is one of only two truly international companies from Australia.'[11] (Confirmation of this strength came with the announcement on September 27, 1988, of pre-tax profits bursting through the billion barrier—$1.05 billion to June 30, indeed second only to BHP—and net profits of $684.8 million, a lift of 72 per cent; the *Australian* headlined: 'Elders heads for No. 1'.) But their eyes are not focused exclusively abroad. Elders is putting up a quarter of the $20 million now being invested in a detailed feasibility study of the Very Fast Train (VFT) which, when built for $4 billion, will take passengers from Melbourne to Sydney in just three hours.[12] The code name for the project is Leap Frog.[13] Such imagination is a promising omen for the next 150 years of Elders IXL.

But in the meantime, keep an eye on those breweries!

Very Fast Train (VFT).

Appendix

The FitzHerbert Converter

Richard FitzHerbert, BSc, FIA, has prepared the following table for the conversion of historic prices to 1988 prices. He offers these explanatory notes by way of introduction:

> The table was prepared using data published in the 1977 *Transactions of the Institute of Actuaries of Australia* (page 560); since 1977, the table is based on data obtained from the Australian Bureau of Statistics.
>
> The basis of conversions is a price index, not a wage index—wage levels are higher now than they were in most of the period covered. There are considerable difficulties, both theoretical and practical, in applying this table, and consequently it gives *approximations* of current-day values—no more.
>
> Example: £15 13s 9d in 1905. Multiply by 2 to convert to decimal currency = $31.38. Multiply by 35 (the factor from the table to cover inflation to bring to 1988 prices) = $1,102.30. Thus, £15 13s 9d in 1905 equates in round figures to $1,100 in 1988.

VALUE OF ONE AUSTRALIAN DOLLAR AT 1988 PRICES

Year	Factor	Year	Factor	Year	Factor	Year	Factor	Year	Factor	Year	Factor	Year	Factor
1860/61	28	1880/81	34	1900/01	36	1920/21	19	1940/41	18	1960/61	6.4	1980/81	1.6
1861/62	28	1881/82	31	1901/02	36	1921/22	20	1941/42	17	1961/62	6.3	1981/82	1.5
1862/63	29	1882/83	32	1902/03	36	1922/23	19	1942/43	16	1962/63	6.2	1982/83	1.3
1863/64	31	1883/84	32	1903/04	35	1923/24	19	1943/44	16	1963/64	6.0	1983/84	1.2
1864/65	31	1884/85	32	1904/05	36	1924/25	18	1944/45	16	1964/65	5.9	1984/85	1.2
1865/66	30	1885/86	33	1905/06	35	1925/26	18	1945/46	16	1965/66	5.7		
1866/67	34	1886/87	35	1906/07	34	1926/27	18	1946/47	15	1966/67	5.5		
1867/68	33	1887/88	33	1907/08	33	1927/28	18	1947/48	14	1967/68	5.4		
1868/69	34	1888/89	32	1908/09	35	1928/29	18	1948/49	13	1968/69	5.2		
1869/70	34	1889/90	32	1909/10	34	1929/30	20	1949/50	12	1969/70	5.0		
1870/71	34	1890/91	35	1910/11	34	1930/31	22	1950/51	9.4	1970/71	4.7		
1871/72	31	1891/92	37	1911/12	31	1931/32	24	1951/52	9.0	1971/72	4.4		
1872/73	30	1892/93	39	1912/13	31	1932/33	24	1952/53	7.9	1972/73	4.0		
1873/74	30	1893/94	41	1913/14	29	1933/34	23	1953/54	7.6	1973/74	3.5		
1874/75	31	1894/95	41	1914/15	27	1934/35	22	1954/55	7.6	1974/75	3.0		
1875/76	31	1895/96	39	1915/16	26	1935/36	21	1955/56	7.4	1975/76	2.6		
1876/77	32	1896/97	38	1916/17	23	1936/37	20	1956/57	6.9	1976/77	2.3		
1877/78	33	1897/98	38	1917/18	22	1937/38	20	1957/58	6.9	1977/78	2.2		
1878/79	33	1898/99	37	1918/19	21	1938/39	20	1958/59	6.9	1978/79	2.0		
1879/80	34	1899/1900	38	1919/20	18	1939/40	19	1959/60	6.6	1979/80	1.8		

Notes

Abbreviations
ADB   *Australian Dictionary of Biography.*
NCSC   National Companies and Securities
           Commission
PRGSSA   *Proceedings of the Royal Geographical Society
           of South Australia*

OVERTURE: FROM A TRICKLE TO A TORRENT
1.   *Minerva* manifest, 1839, in the Mortlock Library of South
     Australiana, Adelaide.
2.   Ibid.
3.   *Gazetteer of the British Isles* (Edinburgh, 1963).
4.   T. Horton Jones, *Six Months in South Australia*
     (London, 1838).
5.   *South Australian Register*, c. 1841.
6.   John Elliott, recorded interview with author, Melbourne, 1988.
7.   Dan Morgan, *Merchants of Grain* (New York, 1979).
8.   Geoffrey Lord, recorded interview with author, Melbourne, 1988.
9.   Ken Jarrett, recorded interview with author, Melbourne, 1988.
10. Tom Kinnison, Kirkcaldy, letter to author, 1988.
11. Elder IXL Annual Report, 1987.
12. *Australian Stock Exchange Journal* (Sydney), March 1974.

CHAPTER 1   BUILDING THE ELDERS EMPIRE
1.   A.J. Harrop, *The Amazing Career of Edward Gibbon Wakefield* (London,
     1928).
2.   C.M.H. Clark, *A History of Australia*, vol. 3 (Melbourne, 1973).
3.   T. Horton Jones, *Six Months in South Australia* (London, 1838).
4.   Paul Maguire, *Australian Journey* (Melbourne, 1942).
5.   G.M. Trevelyan, *English Social History* (London, 1944).
6.   Clark, *History of Australia*, vol. 3.
7.   A.G. Price and J.H. Hammond, *The First Hundred Years* (Adelaide,
     1940).
8.   Ibid.
9.   Fayette Gosse, PRGSSA 63, (1962).
10. Ibid.
11. Rodney Cockburn, *Pastoral Pioneers of South Australia*, vol. 2
     (Adelaide, 1927).
12. Thomas Elder, *Notes from a Pocket Journal of a Trip Up the Murray River,
     1865* (Adelaide, 1893).
13. Gwenda Painter, *The River Trade* (Sydney, 1979).
14. ADB 6, s.v. 'Smith, Robert Barr'.
15. Harold Normandale, *Yorke Peninsula* (Adelaide, 1983).
16. Price and Hammond, *First Hundred Years*.
17. Ibid.
18. Normandale, *Yorke Peninsula*.
19. Price and Hammond, *First Hundred Years*.
20. ADB 6, s.v. 'Smith, Robert Barr'.
21. Cockburn, *Pastoral Pioneers*.
22. Alfred S. Chapman, evidence to the Royal Commission into the
     Pastoral Land Commission, Adelaide, 1891.
23. *Year Book Australia*, 1968.
24. Cockburn, *Pastoral Pioneers*.
25. Thomas Elder, *Narrative of a Tour in Palestine in 1857* (Adelaide,
     1894).
26. Geoffrey Blainey, *A Land Half Won* (Melbourne, 1980).
27. F.E. Baume, *Tragedy Track* (Sydney, 1933).
28. N.E. Phillipson, *Camels in Australia*, PRGSSA, 1895.
29. Blainey, *Land Half Won*.
30. John Ross, *Proceedings of the Royal Geographical Society*, London, 1871.
31. Bessie Threadgill, *South Australian Land Exploration 1856–80*
     (Adelaide, 1922).
32. Blainey, *Land Half Won*.
33. Price and Hammond, *First Hundred Years*.
34. K. Peake-Jones, 'A *Study of Incompatibles*, PRGSSA 85 (1986).

35. *Register* (Adelaide), 1891.
36. N.E. Phillipson, *op. cit.*
37. PRGSSA 11 (1910).
38. Peake-Jones, 'Study of Incompatibles'.
39. Ibid.
40. *South Australian Advertiser*, 29 January 1869.
41. *South Australian Advertiser*, 2 March 1869.
42. National Council of Wool Selling Brokers of Australia, Melbourne,
     1988.
43. Blainey, *Land Half Won*.
44. Clark, *History of Australia*, vol. 3.
45. Price and Hammond, *First Hundred Years*.
46. Alan Barnard, *The Australian Wool Market 1840–1900* (Melbourne,
     1958).
47. ADB 4 s.v. 'Darling, John'.
48. Cockburn, *Pastoral Pioneers*.
49. Robert Barr Smith, Letters, Mortlock Library, Adelaide.
50. Price and Hammond, *First Hundred Years*.
51. Norman Young, 'By Chance I Became a Director of Elders', MS.
     (Adelaide, 1986).
52. Sir Norman Young, recorded interview with author, Adelaide,
     1988.
53. Michael Cannon, *The Land Boomers* (Melbourne, 1966).
54. Robert Darlington, *Land of Hopes and Illusions* (Sydney, 1987).
55. Price and Hammond, *First Hundred Years*.
56. Elder, Smith & Co., Annual Report, 1896.
57. Thomas Elder, *Notes from a Pocket Journal of Rambles in Spain in 1860*
     (Adelaide, 1894).
58. Fayette Gosse.
59. PRGSSA III, (1899).
60. Price and Hammond, *First Hundred Years*.
61. Elder, Smith & Co., Annual Report, 1903.
62. Price and Hammond, *First Hundred Years*.
63. ADB 6, s.v. 'Smith, Robert Barr'.
64. Ibid.
65. Cockburn, *Pastoral Pioneers*; ADB 6, s.v. 'Waite, Peter'.
66. Price and Hammond, *First Hundred Years*.
67. Elder, Smith & Co., Annual Report, 1930.
68. Price and Hammond, *First Hundred Years*.
69. Young, 'By Chance'.
70. Price and Hammond, *First Hundred Years*.
71. Elder, Smith & Co., Annual Reports, 1941–44.
72. *Year Book Australia*, vol. 39 (1953).
73. J.A. Bushnell, *Australian Company Mergers 1946–1959*.
74. Ibid.
75. Former executive A, recorded interview with author, Adelaide,
     1988.
76. Ibid.
77. Ibid.
78. Young, 'By Chance'.
79. Geoffrey Manning, *The Elder Smith Goldsbrough Mort Merger* (Canberra,
     1970).
80. Bushnell, *Australian Company Mergers*.
81. Ibid.
82. Young, 'By Chance'.
83. Ibid.
84. Ibid.
85. *Year Book Australia*, vol. 49 (1963).
86. Manning, *Elder Smith Goldsbrough Mort Merger*.
87. Barnard, *Australian Wool Market*.
88. Bushnell, *Australian Company Mergers*.
89. John Baillieu, recorded interview with author, Melbourne, 1988.
90. Alan Barnard, *Visions and Profits: Studies in the Business Career of
     T.S. Mort* (Melbourne, 1961).
91. Barnard, *Australian Wool Market*.
92. Blainey, *Land Half Won*.
93. E.W. Campbell, *The Sixty Rich Families Who Own Australia* (Sydney,
     1963).
94. Manning, *Elder Smith Goldsbrough Mort Merger*.
95. Ibid.

96. Statement to the Melbourne and Adelaide Stock Exchanges, 23 February 1962.
97. Advertisements in newspapers, 4 April 1962.
98. Norman Young, 'By Chance'.
99. Manning, *Elder Smith Goldsbrough Mort Merger*.
100. Ibid.
101. Ibid.
102. Former executive A, recorded interview with author, 1988.
103. John Hill, recorded interview with author, Melbourne, 1988.
104. Young, 'By Chance'.
105. Alec Morrison, recorded interview with author, Deniliquin, 1988.
106. Former executive A, recorded interview with author, 1988.
107. Ibid.
108. Trevor Sykes, *The Money Miners* (Sydney, 1978).
109. Young, 'By Chance'.
110. Painter, *River Trade*.
111. Elders GM, Annual Report, 1974.
112. Elders GM, Annual Reports, 1976–80.
113. ADB 5 s.v. 'Pitt, George Matcham'.
114. Elders GM, Annual Report, 1976.
115. John Hill, recorded interview with author, 1988.
116. Ibid.
117. Former executive A, recorded interview with author, 1988.
118. Young, 'By Chance'.

CHAPTER 2   THE EXTRAORDINARY 'JAM TIN JONES'

1. Henry Melville, *Van Diemen's Land Annual* (Hobart, 1834).
2. Maitland and Krone, *The Cyclopedia of Tasmania*, vol. 1 (Hobart, 1900).
3. E.W. Campbell, *The Sixty Families Who Own Australia* (Sydney, 1963).
4. John Reynolds, *Sir Henry Jones, KB, PTHRA* (Hobart, 1973).
5. Ibid.
6. Ibid.
7. Ibid. (teachers the Misses F.E. Rule and M. Ogilvy to John Reynolds).
8. Ibid. (Henry Jones to Frederick H. Peacock).
9. Ibid.
10. A.W. Palfreyman, quoted in Melbourne *Sun News-Pictorial*, 11 January 1965.
11. Ibid.
12. *An Act to Constitute the Commonwealth of Australia*, London, 1900.
13. C.E. Sayers, *David Syme, a Life* (Melbourne, 1965).
14. Bryce Fraser, ed., *The Macquarie Book of Events* (Sydney, 1983).
15. NSWA 1885–86.
16. Reynolds, *Sir Henry Jones*.
17. Ibid.
18. Maitland and Krone, *Cyclopedia of Tasmania*.
19. Reynolds, *Sir Henry Jones*.
20. Maitland and Krone, *Cyclopedia of Tasmania*.
21. Ibid.; Reynolds, *Sir Henry Jones*.
22. C.M.H. Clark, *A History of Australia*, vol. V (Melbourne, 1981).
23. Dorothy Morgan, 'A History of the Henry Jones Group of Companies, 1889–1972', MS, Melbourne, 1985.
24. Reynolds, *Sir Henry Jones*.
25. Ibid.; Geoffrey Blainey, *The Rush that Never Ended* (Melbourne, 1963), ADB 10, s.v. 'Miles, Edward Thomas'.
26. Australian Stock Exchange, Hobart, 1988.
27. ADB, vol. 10, s.v. 'Miles, Edward Thomas'.
28. Reynolds, *Sir Henry Jones*.
29. Morgan, 'History of the Henry Jones Group'.
30. Ibid.
31. Ibid.
32. Ibid., Reynolds, *Sir Henry Jones*.
33. Ibid.
34. Ibid.
35. Campbell, *Sixty Families*.
36. Reynolds, *Sir Henry Jones*.
37. Ibid.
38. Henry Jones Co-operative, Annual Report, 1913–14.
39. Imperial Honours List, London, 1919.
40. *Mercury*, 12 November 1915.
41. Henry Jones Co-operative, Annual Report, 1918–19.
42. Morgan, 'History of the Henry Jones Group'.
43. Ibid.
44. C.M.H. Clark, *A History of Australia*, vol. VI (Melbourne, 1987).
45. Morgan, 'History of the Henry Jones Group'.
46. Reynolds, *Sir Henry Jones*.
47. *Huon Times* (Franklin), November 1926.
48. Morgan, 'History of the Henry Jones Group'.
49. A.W. Palfreyman to R.E. Hewat, Melbourne, 1945.
50. Morgan, 'History of the Henry Jones Group'.
51. *Age*, 14 January 1965.
52. Tom Prior, *Sun News-Pictorial*, 11 January 1965.
53. Morgan, 'History of the Henry Jones Group'.
54. Ibid.
55. Peter Denton, *Elliott: A Biography of John D. Elliott* (Sydney, 1987).

CHAPTER 3   THE BEER BARONS UNITE

1. Cyril Pearl, *Beer, Glorious Beer* (Sydney, 1969).
2. Keith Dunstan, *The Amber Nectar* (Melbourne, 1987).
3. Pearl, *Beer, Glorious Beer*.
4. *Australian Brewers' Journal* (Melbourne), 20 April 1887.
5. Dunstan, *Amber Nectar*.
6. Ibid.
7. Michael Cannon, *The Land Boomers* (Melbourne, 1966).
8. C.M.H. Clark, *A History of Australia*, vol. V (Melbourne, 1981).
9. Dunstan, *Amber Nectar*.
10. ADB, vol. 8, s.v. 'Cohen, Montague'.
11. Dunstan, *Amber Nectar*; ADB, vol. 8, s.v. 'de Bavay, Auguste Joseph François'.
12. Geoffrey Blainey, *The Rush That Never Ended* (Melbourne, 1963).
13. ADB, vol. 8, s.v. 'de Bavay, A.J.F.'.
14. Pearl, *Beer, Glorious Beer*.
15. *Australian Brewers' Journal*, June–July 1897.
16. *What's Brewing* (Melbourne) 17, no. 1 (March 1966).
17. Dunstan, *Amber Nectar*; *Year Book Australia*, vol. 54 (1968).
18. Dunstan, *Amber Nectar*.
19. Ibid.
20. ABD, vol. 8, s.v. 'de Bavay, A.J.F.'.
21. Freda Irving, *Weekend Australian*, 20–21 April 1983.
22. ADB, vol. 7, s.v. 'Baillieu, William Lawrence'.
23. Ibid.
24. Ibid.
25. Cannon, *Land Boomers*.
26. ADB, vol. 7, s.v. 'Baillieu, W.L.'.
27. E.W. Campbell, *The Sixty Rich Families Who Own Australia* (Sydney, 1963).
28. ADB, vol. 7, s.v. 'Baillieu, W.L.'.
29. Dunstan, *Amber Nectar*.
30. ADB, vol. 8, s.v. 'Cohen, Montague'; *Weekend Australian*, 20–21 April 1983; Dunstan, *Amber Nectar*; ADB, vol. 7, s.v. 'Baillieu, W.L.'; Blainey, *Rush That Never Ended*.
31. Dunstan, *Amber Nectar*; Blainey, *Rush That Never Ended*.
32. ADB, vol. 8, s.v. 'de Bavay, A.J.F.'.
33. Dunstan, *Amber Nectar*.
34. Minutes of CUB, 8 April 1925.
35. Dunstan, *Amber Nectar*.
36. Ibid.; *What's Brewing* 17, no. 1.
37. Paul Ormonde, recorded interview with author, Melbourne, 1988.
38. Ibid.
39. *Sun News-Pictorial*, 10 October 1968.
40. *Australian*, 30 October 1969.
41. Barry Humphries, *The Wonderful World of Barry McKenzie* (Melbourne, 1968).
42. Dunstan, *Amber Nectar*.
43. Ormonde recorded interview with author, 1988.

CHAPTER 4   JOHN ELLIOTT LAUNCHES HIS TEAM

1. Trevor Kennedy, *Top Guns* (Melbourne, 1988).
2. John Elliott's birth certificate.
3. Peter Denton, *Elliott: A Biography of John D. Elliott* (Sydney, 1986).
4. Ibid.
5. Nancy Roper, *Nurse's Dictionary* (London, 1973).
6. Denton, *Elliott*.
7. Ibid.

8. Ibid.
9. John Elliott, recorded interview with author, Melbourne, 1988.
10. Kennedy, *Top Guns*.
11. Denton, *Elliott*.
12. Noel Voight to Denton, in *Elliott*.
13. John Elliott, recorded interview with author, Melbourne, 1988.
14. Ibid.
15. Denton, *Elliott*.
16. Michael Shanks, *The Innovators* (London, 1967).
17. John Naisbitt, *Megatrends* (New York, 1982).
18. Denton, *Elliott*.
19. Ibid.
20. C. Northcote Parkinson, *The Director* (London, 1960).
21. Tony Thomas and Julietta Jameson, *Business Review Weekly*, 1 May 1987.
22. Sir Roderick Carnegie, recorded interview with author, Melbourne, 1988.
23. Mary L. Shelman, *Elders IXL Ltd* (Harvard, 1987).
24. Ibid.
25. John Elliott, recorded interview with author, 1988.
26. Sir Roderick Carnegie, recorded interview with author, 1988.
27. Shanks, *Innovators*.
28. Peter Scanlon, recorded interview with author, Melbourne, 1988.
29. Denton, *Elliott*.
30. Ibid.
31. Elliott to Kennedy, in *Top Guns*.
32. Elliott to Denton, in *Elliott*.
33. Alan Reid, *The Gorton Experiment* (Sydney, 1971).
34. John Elliott, recorded interview with author, 1988.
35. Ibid.
36. Sir Roderick Carnegie, recorded interview with author, 1988.
37. John Elliott, recorded interview with author, 1988.
38. Quoted by J. Elliott.
39. Shelman, *Elders IXL Ltd*.
40. John Elliott, 'Taking Tiger by the Tail' (Melbourne, 1972).
41. Shelman, *Elders IXL Ltd*.
42. *Age*, 29 June 1972.
43. Elliott, 'Tiger by the Tail'.
44. Denton, *Elliott*.
45. Dorothy Morgan, 'A History of the Henry Jones Group of Companies, 1889–1972', MS, Melbourne, 1985.
46. Quoted by John Elliott.
47. Denton, *Elliott*.
48. Shelman, *Elders IXL Ltd*.
49. *Age*, 25 September 1972.
50. Tim Hewat, *The Blues* (Melbourne, 1982).
51. Denton, *Elliott*.
52. *Herald* (Melbourne), 27 September 1972.
53. *Australian Financial Review*, 10 November 1972.
54. Barbara A'Beckett, recorded interview with author, Melbourne, 1988.
55. Peter Scanlon, recorded interview with author, 1988.
56. Barbara A'Beckett, recorded interview with author, 1988.
57. Shelman, *Elders IXL Ltd*.
58. John Elliott to Michael Macgeorge, the *Age*, 29 August 1974.
59. Geoff Lord, recorded interview with author, Melbourne, 1988.
60. Ibid.
61. Ken Jarrett, recorded interview with author, Melbourne, 1988.
62. Ibid.
63. Paul Ormonde, recorded interview with author, Melbourne, 1988.
64. John Elliott to Michael Macgeorge.
65. Elliott, 'Tiger by the Tail'.
66. Denton, *Elliott*.
67. John Elliott, recorded interview with author, 1988.
68. Neil Hunter, recorded interview with author, Bendigo, 1988.
69. *Australian*, 6 March, 1973.
70. *Australian Financial Review*, 29 March 1973.
71. *Australian*, 17 April 1973.
72. Henry Jones IXL, 63rd Annual Report (1973).
73. Ibid.
74. Ibid.
75. John Elliott, recorded interview with author, 1988.
76. Denton, *Elliott*.
77. John Elliott to Michael Cosgrove.
78. Ibid.
79. *Herald* (Melbourne), 3 July 1973.
80. Henry Jones IXL, 64th Annual Report (1974).
81. Ibid.
82. Sir Roderick Carnegie, recorded interview with author, 1988.
83. Kennedy, *Top Guns*.
84. John Elliott, recorded interview with author, 1988.
85. Henry Jones IXL, 65th Annual Report (1975).
86. *National Times*, 24 March 1975.
87. Kennedy, *Top Guns*.
88. Peter Scanlon, recorded interview with author, 1988.
89. Gough Whitlam, *The Whitlam Government 1972–1975* (Melbourne, 1985).
90. John Elliott, recorded interview with author, 1988.
91. Barbara A'Beckett, recorded interview with author, 1988.
92. Geoff Lord, recorded interview with author, 1988.
93. Robert Gottliebsen, *Business Review Weekly*, 4 April 1981.
94. *Sun News-Pictorial*, 11 February 1976.
95. *Australian Financial Review*, 11 February 1976.
96. Denton, *Elliott*.
97. Peter Scanlon, recorded interview with author, 1988.
98. Henry Jones IXL, 67th Annual Report (1977).
99. *Age*, 21 September 1976.
100. *Australian Financial Review*, 5 July 1977.
101. *Murrumbidgee Irrigator* (Griffith), 5 July 1977.
102. *Australian*, 4 August 1977.
103. Quoted by Elliott.
104. John Elliott, recorded interview with author, 1988.
105. Barbara A'Beckett, recorded interview with author, 1988.
106. *Australian*, 9 December 1977.
107. *Age*, 12 July 1979.
108. *Sun News-Pictorial*, 12 June 1979.
109. Henry Jones IXL, 71st Annual Report (1981).
110. Henry Jones IXL, 70th Annual Report (1980).
111. *Sun News-Pictorial*, 9 October 1979.
112. Kennedy, *Top Guns*.
113. Denton, *Elliott*.
114. Geoff Lord, recorded interview with author, 1988.
115. Ibid.
116. Henry Jones IXL, 71st Annual Report.
117. Ibid.
118. Ibid.
119. Barbara A'Beckett and Peter Scanlon, recorded interview with author, 1988.
120. Denton, *Elliott*.
121. *Age*, 5 December 1980.
122. *Business Review Weekly*, 4 April 1981.
123. David Uren, the *Age*, 5 December 1980.
124. John Baillieu, recorded interview with author, Melbourne, 1988.

CHAPTER 5   THE BIRTH OF MANAGEMENT TAKEOVERS

1. Quoted by Gregory Hywood in the *Australian Financial Review*, 4 March 1988.
2. *Business Review Weekly*, 3 October 1986.
3. Ibid.
4. J.W. von Doussa, QC, *First Interim Report* (Adelaide, 1982).
5. Ibid.
6. Ibid.
7. Ibid.
8. Elders GM Annual Reports, 1974–81.
9. Von Doussa, *First Interim Report*; Sir Norman Young, 'By Chance I Become a Director of Elders', MS, Adelaide, 1986.
10. Von Doussa, *First Interim Report*.
11. Ibid.
12. Ibid.
13. Young, 'By Chance'.
14. Sir Norman Young, recorded interview with author, Adelaide, 1988.
15. Young, 'By Chance'.
16. Ibid.
17. Peter Scanlon, recorded interview with author, Melbourne, 1988.
18. Ibid.
19. Ibid.

164

20. Von Doussa, *First Interim Report*.
21. Peter Scanlon, recorded interview with author, 1988.
22. Ibid.
23. Von Doussa, *First Interim Report*.
24. Young, 'By Chance'.
25. Von Doussa, *First Interim Report*.
26. Ibid.
27. Peter Scanlon and Bob Cowper, report for Henry Jones board, Melbourne, March 1981.
28. Peter Scanlon, recorded interview with author, 1988.
29. Ibid.
30. Von Doussa, *First Interim Report*.
31. *Business Review Weekly*, 26 September 1986.
32. Peter Scanlon, recorded interview with author, 1988.
33. Ibid.
34. Young, 'By Chance'; von Doussa, *First Interim Report*.
35. Sir Ian McLennan, recorded interview with author, Melbourne, 1988.
36. Peter Scanlon, recorded interview with author, 1988.
37. John Elliott, recorded interview with author, Melbourne, 1988.
38. Peter Denton, *Elliott* (Sydney, 1986).
39. Elders GM Annual Report, 1981.
40. Von Doussa, *First Interim Report*.
41. Young, 'By Chance'.
42. Ibid.
43. Ibid.
44. Sir Ian McLennan, recorded interview with author, 1988.
45. Press release, Adelaide and Melbourne, 30 March 1981.
46. Sir Norman Young, recorded interview with author, 1988.
47. Geoff Lord, recorded interview with author, Melbourne, 1988.
48. Henry Jones IXL, 71st Annual Report (1980); Elders IXL, Annual Report, 1982.
49. Sir Ian McLennan, recorded interview with author, 1988.
50. John Elliott, recorded interview with author, 1988.
51. John Elliott and Charles Faggotter, recorded interviews with author, Melbourne, 1988.
52. Elders IXL Annual Report, 1982.
53. Trevor Griffin, Instrument of Appointment of Inspector, Adelaide 1981.
54. Von Doussa, *First Interim Report*.
55. Ibid.
56. Ibid.
57. Elders IXL Annual Reports, 1982, 1983.
58. John Elliott, recorded interview with author, 1988.
59. Ibid.
60. Ibid.
61. Elders IXL Annual Report, 1982.
62. Denton, *Elliott*.
63. Ibid.
64. Elders IXL Annual Report, 1982.
65. Geoff Lord, recorded interview with author, 1988.
66. John Elliott, recorded interview with author, 1988.
67. Ibid.
68. Ibid.
69. Ibid.
70. Quoted by Charles Wright in *Australian Business* (Sydney), 2 September 1987.
71. Ibid.
72. Denton, *Elliott*.
73. Michael Nugent, recorded interview with author, Melbourne, 1988.
74. Ibid.
75. Michael Peck, interview with author, Melbourne, 1988.
76. Pamela Lewers, interview with author, Melbourne, 1988.
77. Michael Peck, interview with author, 1988.
78. Elders IXL Annual Report, 1984.

CHAPTER 6   THE BEER BARREL POLKA

1. *Business Review Weekly*, 26 September 1986.
2. Ronald Brierley, press conference, Windsor Hotel, Melbourne, 30 November 1983.
3. *Business Review Weekly*, 14 August 1987.
4. Peter Denton, *Elliott* (Sydney, 1986).
5. Keith Dunstan, *The Amber Nectar* (Melbourne, 1987).

6. *Business Review Weekly*, 15 August 1986.
7. Dunstan, *Amber Nectar*.
8. Denton, *Elliott*.
9. John Elliott, recorded interviews with author, 1988.
10. Denton, *Elliott*.
11. *Age*, 1 December 1983.
12. CUB press release, 30 November 1983.
13. CUB press release, 2 December 1983.
14. *Age*, 6 December 1983.
15. John Elliott, recorded interview with author, 1988.
16. Denton, *Elliott*.
17. *Age*, 14 January 1984.
18. John Baillieu, recorded interview with author, Melbourne, 1988.
19. Denton, *Elliott*.
20. Dunstan, *Amber Nectar*.
21. Ibid.
22. Ken Jarrett, recorded interview with author, Melbourne, 1988.
23. Dunstan, *Amber Nectar*.
24. Ibid.
25. Denton, *Elliott*.
26. John Elliott, recorded interview with author, 1988.
27. Ibid.
28. Elders IXL Annual Report, 1984.
29. Ibid.
30. John Elliott, *The Need for Deregulation in Australia* (Melbourne, 1984).
31. *Age*, 4 May 1985.
32. Trevor Kennedy, *Top Guns* (Sydney, 1988).
33. Geoff Lord, recorded interview with author, Melbourne, 1988.
34. Dunstan, *Amber Nectar*.
35. Geoff Lord, recorded interview with author, 1988.
36. John Baillieu, recorded interview with author, 1988.
37. Paul Ormonde, recorded interview with author, Melbourne, 1988.
38. Ibid.
39. Ibid.
40. Dunstan, *Amber Nectar*.
41. Denton, *Elliott*.
42. Elders IXL Annual Report, 1985.

CHAPTER 7   GLOBALISING FOSTER'S

1. Henry Bosch, C.M. Williams, and A.B. Greenwood, National Companies and Securities Commission Report on the Cross Investment between The Broken Hill Proprietary Company Limited and Elders IXL Limited (NCSC Report), Melbourne, September 1986.
2. Elders IXL Annual Report, 1985.
3. Keith Dunstan, *The Amber Nectar* (Melbourne, 1987).
4. *Australian Business*, 2 October 1985.
5. Peter Denton, *Elliott* (Sydney, 1986).
6. Ibid.
7. John Elliott, recorded interview with author, Melbourne, 1988.
8. Dunstan, *Amber Nectar*.
9. *The Times*, 22 October 1985.
10. Dunstan, *Amber Nectar*.
11. Paul Ormonde, recorded interview with author, Melbourne, 1988.
12. Geoff Lord, recorded interview with author, Melbourne, 1988.
13. Ken Jarrett, recorded interview with author, Melbourne, 1988.
14. Dunstan, *Amber Nectar*.
15. NCSC Report.
16. John Elliott, recorded interview with author, 1988.
17. NCSC Report.
18. John Elliott, recorded interview with author, 1988.
19. NCSC Report.
20. Ibid.
21. Ibid.
22. Gideon Haigh, *The Battle for BHP* (Melbourne, 1987).
23. Elders IXL Annual Report, 1986.
24. NCSC Report.
25. Ibid.
26. *Australian Financial Review*, 14 March 1986.
27. *Sun News-Pictorial*, 14 March 1986.
28. John Elliott, recorded interview with author, 1988.
29. Haigh, *Battle for BHP*.
30. John Elliott, recorded interview with author, 1988; NCSC Report.

31. Haigh, *Battle for BHP*; NCSC Report.
32. NCSC Report; Keith Dunstan, *Amber Nectar*.
33. Haigh, *Battle for BHP*.
34. Ibid.
35. NCSC Report.
36. Ibid.
37. Ibid.
38. Haigh, *Battle for BHP*.
39. NCSC Report.
40. Ibid.
41. *Australian Business*, 13 July 1988.
42. *Business Review Weekly*, 14 August 1987.
43. NCSC Report.
44. Haigh, *Battle for BHP*.
45. Dunstan, *Amber Nectar*.
46. NCSC Report.
47. Haigh, *Battle for BHP*.
48. Ibid.
49. Elders IXL Annual Report, 1986.
50. John Elliott, recorded interview with author, 1988.
51. Peter Scanlon to the NCSC, NCSC Report.
52. John Elliott, recorded interview with author, 1988.
53. Dunstan, *Amber Nectar*.
54. Denton, *Elliott*.
55. Elders IXL Annual Report, 1987.
56. Ibid.
57. Ibid.
58. Haigh, *Battle for BHP*.
59. *Australian Financial Review*, 2 June 1988.
60. *Business Review Weekly*, 17 June 1988.
61. Dunstan, *Amber Nectar*.
62. Paul Ormonde, interview with author, 1988.
63. Andrew Cummins quoted in *Business Review Weekly*, 20 May 1988.
64. Sir Roderick Carnegie, recorded interview with author, Melbourne, 1988.
65. Matthew Stevens, *Business Review Weekly*, 20 May 1988.
66. Ibid.
67. Ibid.
68. David Tomlinson, the *Financial Australian*, 13 May 1988.
69. John Elliott, recorded interview with author, 1988.
70. Quoted by James McCullough, the *Financial Australian*, 22 June 1988.
71. Ibid.
72. Matthew Stevens, *Business Review Weekly*, 6 May 1988.
73. Matthew Stevens, *Business Review Weekly*, 17 June 1988.
74. *Wall Street Journal — Europe*, 1 June 1988.
75. *Australian Financial Review*, 2 June 1988.
76. *Australian Financial Review*, 14 June 1988.
77. *Australian*, 10 June 1988.
78. Elders IXL Annual Report, 1987.

CHAPTER 8   THE EMPIRE STRIKES OUTWARDS

1.   John Elliott, recorded interview with author, Melbourne, 1988.
2.   *Australian Financial Review* price quote November 1987, July 1988.
3.   Elders IXL Annual Report, 1987.
4.   Ken Jarrett, recorded interview with author, Melbourne, 1988.
5.   Elders Finance Group, Annual Report, 1987.
6.   Ibid; Elders IXL Annual Report, 1987.
7.   Elders Finance Group, Annual Report, 1987.
8.   Matthew Stevens, *Business Review Weekly*, 24 June 1988.
9.   Ibid.
10. Patricia Howard, the *Age*, 30 July 1988.
11. Ken Jarrett, recorded interview with author, 1988.
12. Michael Nugent, recorded interview with author, Melbourne, 1988.
13. Elders IXL Annual Report, 1984.
14. Michael Nugent, recorded interview with author, 1988.
15. Michael Hamilton, recorded interview with author, Adelaide, 1988.
16. Charles Faggotter, recorded interview with author, 1988.
17. Michael Nugent, recorded interview with author, 1988.
18. Michael Hamilton, recorded interview with author, 1988.
19. Michael Nugent, recorded interview with author, 1988.
20. Ibid.
21. Ibid.
22. Ibid.
23. *Australian Financial Review*, 8 July 1988.
24. Michael Nugent, recorded interview with author, 1988.
25. Ibid.
26. Dan Morgan, *Merchants of Grain* (New York, 1979).
27. Michael Nugent, recorded interview with author, 1988.
28. Geoff Lord, recorded interview with author, Melbourne, 1988.
29. Michael Hamilton, recorded interview with author, 1988.
30. Geoff Lord, recorded interview with author, 1988.
31. Graeme Jones, the *Australian*, 17–18 June 1988.
32. John Tilston, *Australian Financial Review*, 26 August 1988.
33. John Elliott, recorded interview with author, 1988.
34. *Herald*, 26 August 1988.
35. Geoff Lord, recorded interview with author, 1988.
36. Graeme Jones, the *Australian*, 22 April 1988.
37. Shirley Skeel, *Australian Business*, 8 June 1988.
38. Peter Scanlon, recorded interview with author, Melbourne, 1988.

CHAPTER 9   POLITICS, BUSINESS, FOOTBALL

1.   Barbara A'Beckett, recorded interview with author, Melbourne, 1988.
2.   *Business Review Weekly*, 27 May 1988.
3.   Donald Greenlees, the *Weekend Australian*, 18–19 June 1988.
4.   Channel Nine News, Melbourne, 15 June 1988; Geoff Kitney, *Australian Financial Review*, 16 June 1988.
5.   John Elliott, speech to Young Presidents' Organisation, Melbourne, 1988.
6.   John Elliott, recorded interview with author, Melbourne, 1988.
7.   Robert Gordon Menzies, *Afternoon Light* (Melbourne, 1967).
8.   Ibid.
9.   Ibid.
10. John Elliott, recorded interviews with author, 1988.
11. Paraphrased from Abraham Lincoln (1809–65).
12. John Elliott, recorded interview with author, 1988.
13. Derek Denton, interview with author, Melbourne, 1988.
14. *Lloyds Register of Shipping* (London, 1988).
15. 3LO, Melbourne, 14 June 1988.
16. 3LO, Melbourne, 17 June 1988.
17. 3LO, Melbourne, 1 August 1988.
18. Ben Potter's 'Bourse Sauce', *Australian Financial Review*, 31 May 1988.
19. Trevor Kennedy, *Top Guns* (Sydney, 1988).
20. Graeme Beck, recorded interview with author, Deniliquin, 1988.
21. Ibid.
22. Jenny Brown, 'Home' in the *Age*, 12 July 1988.
23. Julie Dillon, *New Idea*, 9 July 1988.
24. Elders IXL Annual Report, 1988.

RONDO: TO THE VICTOR BELONG THE SPOILS

1.   Elders share price 1 August 1988.
2.   'Rich 200', *Business Review Weekly*, 14 August 1987; 'Australia's Richest 300', *Australian Business*, 13 July 1988.
3.   Geoff Lord, recorded interview with author, Melbourne, 1988.
4.   Bryan Frith, the *Weekend Australian*, 7–8 May 1988.
5.   John McIntosh, *Unlimited Success on the Stock Exchange* (Melbourne, 1987).
6.   Peter Scanlon, recorded interview with author, Melbourne, 1988.
7.   John Elliott, recorded interview with author, Melbourne, 1988.
8.   Geoff Lord, recorded interview with author, 1988.
9.   Ali Cromie, *Business Review Weekly*, 26 August 1988.
10. John Baillieu, recorded interview with author, Melbourne, 1988.
11. John Elliott, recorded interview with author, 1988.
12. Barrie Dunstan, *Australian Financial Review*, 15 June 1988.
13. Ben Potter, *Australian Financial Review*, 17 June 1988.

Index